NO.11, SPRING 1999

NEW DIRECTIONS FOR SCHOOL LEADERSHIP

Reflections of First-Year Teachers on School Culture

Questions, Hopes, and Challenges

REBECCA VAN DER BOGERT

Winnetka Public Schools, Evanston, Illinois

EDITOR-IN-CHIEF

MORGAEN L. DONALDSON

Boston Arts Academy

BRIAN POON

Brookline High School

EDITORS

REFLECTIONS OF FIRST-YEAR TEACHERS ON SCHOOL CULTURE:
QUESTIONS, HOPES, AND CHALLENGES
Morgaen L. Donaldson, Brian Poon (eds.)
New Directions for School Leadership, No. 11, Spring 1999
Rebecca van der Bogert, Editor-in-Chief

Microfilm copies of issues and articles are available in 16 mm and 35 mm, as well as microfiche in 105 mm, through University Microfilms Inc., 300 North Zeeb Road, Ann Arbor, Michigan 48106-1346.

ISSN 1089-5612   ISBN 0-7879-4701-6

NEW DIRECTIONS FOR SCHOOL LEADERSHIP is part of The Jossey-Bass Education Series and is published quarterly by Jossey-Bass Inc., Publishers, 350 Sansome Street, San Francisco, California 94104-1342.

SUBSCRIPTIONS: Please see Back Issue/Subscription Order Form at the back of this issue.

EDITORIAL CORRESPONDENCE should be sent to Rebecca van der Bogert, Winnetka Public Schools, 2759 Eastwood Avenue, Evanston, Illinois 60201.

Jossey-Bass Web address: www.josseybass.com

Printed in the United States of America on acid-free recycled paper containing 100 percent recovered waste paper, of which at least 20 percent is postconsumer waste.

The International Network of Principals' Centers

The International Network of Principals' Centers sponsors *New Directions for School Leadership* as part of its commitment to strengthening leadership at the individual school level through professional development for leaders. The network has a membership of principals' centers, academics, and practitioners in the United States and overseas and is open to all groups and institutions committed to the growth of school leaders and the improvement of schools. The Network currently functions primarily as an information exchange and support system for member centers in their efforts to work directly with school leaders in their communities. Its office is in the Principals' Center at the Harvard Graduate School of Education.

The Network offers these services:

- The International Directory of Principals' Centers features member centers with contact persons, descriptions of center activities, program references, and evaluation instruments.
- The Annual Conversation takes place every spring, when members meet for seminars, workshops, speakers, and to initiate discussions that will continue throughout the year.
- *Newsnotes*, the Network's quarterly newsletter, informs members of programs, conferences, workshops, and special interest items.
- *Reflections*, the annual journal, includes articles by principals, staff developers, university educators, and principals' center staff members.

For further information, please contact:

International Network of Principals' Centers
Harvard Graduate School of Education
336 Gutman Library
Cambridge, MA 02138
(617) 495–9812

Contents

Foreword

AT AN EARLIER time in our history, in particular in the latter part of the nineteenth century and the early years of the twentieth century, those who wrote most authoritatively about teaching and learning practice in schools were classroom teachers. Out of those accounts grew the understanding that theory and practice were reciprocal, fully integrated formulations. In the middle to later years of the twentieth century, however, writing about classroom practice has tended to move away from schools and almost exclusively into colleges and universities. In the process, it has become less interesting to classroom teachers, often labeled by them as "theoretical" and seen as disconnected from critical practice. Refreshingly, we are witnessing changes in the literature on classroom practice as observers, researchers, biographers, and writers. *Reflections of First-Year Teachers on School Culture: Questions, Hopes, and Challenges* is an example of this kind of change around collaborative work emanating from schools.

At the heart of the accounts in this text, essentially reflections on the first year of teaching, is the belief that there is much to gain, as well as share, from serious reflection on practice, on the experience of the teaching-learning exchange in a school setting. The writers, Marco Curnen, Morgaen L. Donaldson, Kelly Klinefelter Lee, Allyson Mizoguchi, and Brian Poon entered their first years as teachers committed to reflective practice. They believed, as individuals and collectively, that this first year was important, a genuine marking time, the beginning of a career that mattered to them. They didn't want to lose its significance symbolically or literally. And I encouraged them to believe that their stories would matter to others.

I should note that the five writers were all members of the same teacher education cohort at the Harvard Graduate School of Education. I was privileged to work with them in a program filled with idealism, marked by some of the following beliefs: teaching is truly a profession of hope; teaching should be thought about in terms of possibilities; students in schools, wherever they are, have many strengths that need to be the starting point for all instruction; a curriculum directed toward inquiry and student understanding of critical ideas/knowledge, marked by a performance view of learning, is attainable; powerful student learning should be expected; reflection on practice is critical; ongoing writing is a means of keeping track of practice; collaborative work enlarges thought; context always matters; and education is always about democracy, that ongoing concern for equity, social justice, respect for difference, and human dignity. I cite the foregoing, abbreviated set of aspirations to provide a context for these particular first-year accounts of teaching.

The five writers entered teaching filled with large hopes. They genuinely believed their work with young people in the schools was important. They also believed they would profit greatly from ongoing collective conversation about their work. They came together regularly through their first year of teaching—sharing journal accounts, posing questions, listening to one another's stories of successful work and ongoing dilemmas. They gained strength from one another, even as they were often discouraged by aspects of their experience. As the year progressed, they came to believe that each of them had a story to tell that would be instructive personally, a kind of reflection that would enable them to make sense of the year. They also came to accept my belief that their stories would be instructive to others.

The accounts that appear are clearly first-year teacher stories. In this regard, there is considerable self-criticism, a good deal of self-doubt, and innumerable questions. But they are, as well, more than that. They speak to what it means to be passionate about teaching practice, to hold onto ideals, to struggle and go on. It is obviously their passion that keeps them going.

Because the stories are meant to convey personal, situated reflections, they are not uniform. The differences, in fact, are striking. Though there are stories of success, there are also stories of doubt. Teaching is difficult. This comes through. The structures and teaching-learning climate of schools are not always conducive to the kinds of idealism these particular teachers entered with. Schools are not always filled with the seriousness of purpose these young teachers sought. Nonetheless, the stories never lapse into despair. Hopefulness is always present. "Teaching as struggle" is present, as is "teaching as inspiration." That teaching is personal is manifest in a large way.

We are in a period in our history when the public discourse is filled with accounts about a crisis in teacher quality. The five teachers whose stories are represented in this text, and many, many others like them, are by every account the persons we need in the schools. They are intelligent, well educated, culturally sensitive, socially committed, filled with idealism, believing that young people in the schools can be powerful learners, capable of changing the world, helping make a democratic life more possible. Moreover, they have the pedagogical skills and understandings necessary to fulfill such larger ends. Knowing them, they put in long days and weeks. Their commitments to their students were overwhelming. Why then were their experiences so difficult?

Are schools, organized as they are, supportive of teachers with the aspirations of the five writers represented in this text? Are they centers of inquiry, of collaboration? Do they encourage ongoing idealism? I remain convinced that if schools are not intellectually vibrant places for students and teachers, settings that foster collaboration and change, they are not going to attract over the long run the kinds of teachers we need. Public policy should focus on ways of helping schools become such vital centers. To do so would be truly revolutionary.

We see in the experience of the five teachers represented in this text different kinds of schools. Most are too large. They weren't intentional centers for collaboration. In several, they seemed resistant to engaging students intensively. They weren't universally supportive of more cooperative practices or greater levels of personalization. They didn't engage these young teachers in particularly supportive ways. They were probably, in these respects, typical of the schools that exist. But we should want more from the schools. One might argue, of course, that the struggles Marco, Kelly, Morgaen, Allyson, and Brian went through in their respective settings were little more than what first-year teachers everywhere experience. The fact is, however, that they expected more. I think they should have expected more. Possibly their writing will contribute to more supportive school environments for other new teachers.

My hope for this text is that it will inspire those in schools and across schools to join together to reflect on their practice and engage in classroom research and writing, becoming in the process the "students of teaching" John Dewey wrote so much about. Students of teaching come together on a regular basis in an effort to enlarge their personal and collective understandings of students' thinking and growth as learners. They are persons who develop and maintain a reflective capacity, becoming in the process clear about their intentions and able to make independent judgments about their classrooms. It is out of such communities of learning that situated writing—rooted in actual schools and classrooms—will become more common, inspiring more fully the movement toward reform in the schools.

I continue to be involved with the five teachers. Kelly is staying home with her new baby but continues to think about teaching. The other four, Morgaen, Marco, Allyson, and Brian are having "better" years. They remain thoughtful about their work, still finding ways to be in collaboration. They are continuing in the journey they began when they entered the Harvard Education program, becoming slowly but surely the students of teaching they wish to be. The schools are better for their presence. Their students are the beneficiaries of their enthusiasm and commitment. Knowing that such thoughtful individuals are entering teaching and working at the task with such energy is inspiring, causing me to be optimistic about the future.

Vito Perrone

VITO PERRONE *is a faculty member in the Harvard Graduate School of Education, where he is also director of programs in teacher education. He has been a public school teacher, a university professor in history, education, and peace studies, and has written extensively about teachers and schools.*

Morgaen and Brian paint a vivid picture of the gatherings they shared with their colleagues during the first year of teaching. These proved to be a support for survival and a community in which to grow. You'll want to join them on their journey as they share their experiences throughout this journal.

1

An invitation to reflection, mulled cider, and honest emotions

Morgaen L. Donaldson, Brian Poon

IT WAS AN unseasonably warm January Saturday. Marco, after attending his daughter's soccer game, arrived by bicycle. Seven months pregnant, Kelly brought a tray of delicious pastries and a sample of her savory writing. Allyson arrived breathless, needlessly apologizing for her tardiness and wielding a stack of scribbled notes. We, Brian and Morgaen, began the discussion by introducing our vision and impetus for organizing this meeting.

We were reuniting as friends and colleagues from Harvard Graduate School of Education's certification program seeking to create a forum for first-year teachers. Each of us had taught in public schools in the Greater Boston area for three months. Through brief phone messages and harried e-mails, we had shared the growing frustrations of first year teaching. As the weeks passed, these intermittent exchanges became insufficient. To varying degrees, all

NEW DIRECTIONS FOR SCHOOL LEADERSHIP, NO. 11, SPRING 1999 © JOSSEY-BASS PUBLISHERS

of us found ourselves teaching in isolation without the mechanisms to reflect on our situations and effectively strategize to improve them. We needed time together to reconnect to the values and missions that induced our entry into the teaching profession.

That Saturday morning was the first of several gatherings devoted to reflecting on our purpose and progress as teachers. To structure our meetings and focus our writing, we generated essential questions. Queries such as, "What were the ideas you had before teaching and how have they played out?" and "Where do you predict your school to be in five years?" provided the touchstones for the first few meetings. These questions ultimately generated many more. Two prominent questions were, "How has your school affected you?" and "How have you affected your school?"

From their inception, these interchanges about teaching and learning proved crucial to our practice. We needed to talk candidly about the pains and joys of first-year teaching. We needed to voice our opinions and frustrations and receive compassionate support and advice. In this spirit, our gatherings were full of emotion. All of us felt as though we were failing to achieve our pedagogical goals. On several occasions, some of us succumbed to despair when describing the conditions under which we worked. We shed tears regularly, and profanities riddled the air. Our meetings, however, also spawned laughter and joy. At the most basic level, our triumphs outweighed our defeats. In the company of people we respected and loved, we celebrated teaching as a noble calling.

In deepening our discourse, writing came to occupy an integral position. The discipline of writing focused our thoughts and allowed us to see lucidly our struggles and potential avenues for improvement. Writing journals gave us a concrete vision of our development as teachers. Individually, each of us could compare our efforts in January with those in May, and glean both subtle and substantial changes. On a collective level, sharing our reflections created a community among us. Our sense of isolation and the uniqueness of our challenges dissipated slowly but perceptibly in this environment. Allyson, for instance, could provide a possible solution for the problem that had stymied Marco for months. Most significantly, sharing our reflections convinced us that we were not alone and that our stories could provoke action.

Though our meetings brought us relief and encouragement, we struggled to find time to write, meet, and reflect. Teaching in the manner we had adopted consumes vast quantities of time and energy. Finding a Saturday in which Kelly was not caring for her newborn, Marco was not tending to family matters, or Allyson was not coaching soccer required monumental effort. Morgaen and Brian encountered difficulty organizing these meetings despite our individual and collective commitment to reflection. Teaching, the interchange between the student and adult in the classroom, was the priority for each one of us.

Ultimately, however, we created time because we came to understand that writing and reflection are not a luxury but a necessity. To the student of teaching, reflection and thoughtful discourse cannot occupy a peripheral position; it must be central and continuous. With this realization, we compiled this collective response to the two questions our conversation repeatedly unearthed: How have you affected your school? and How has your school affected you?

As you read the following stories, envision a warm, wood-paneled room bathed in sunlight and filled with the scent of mulling cider. Picture each of us sprawled on the couch or the floor, engrossed in another person's personal reflection. Imagine the exclamations bubbling from various corners of the room: "Is it really like that in Chelsea? . . . Wow, Brian. . . . This is incredible, Morgaen. . . . I love to read your writing, Allyson. . . . Marco, there's so much love in your story."

We invite you to fill your own mug with cider and join us in imbibing both the joys and sorrows of five first-year teachers.

MORGAEN L. DONALDSON *teaches humanities at the Boston Arts Academy, a public high school for the arts in Boston, Massachusetts. During the 1997–1998 year, she taught history, government, and global studies at Framingham High School in Framingham, Massachusetts. She graduated from Princeton University in 1994, taught English at a university in Northern Thailand, and obtained a master's degree from Harvard Graduate School of Education in 1997.*

BRIAN POON *is presently teaching philosophy, gender studies, and world history at Brookline High School in Brookline, Massachusetts. Before beginning his Sisyphean offensive against Brookline's cafeteria in the fall of 1997, Brian attended the Harvard Graduate School of Education. Prior to graduate school, he served as assistant director of admission for three years at his alma mater, Haverford College.*

Teaching can be messy, fraught with ambiguity and inexactitude. Instead of trying to "neaten" her classes by instituting standardized curricular measures or establishing authoritarian discipline, Kelly learned that she needed to wrestle with the uncertainties in teaching. She embraced this struggle even as she encountered institutional resistance to her methods and philosophy. To Kelly, teaching is necessarily both arduous and cluttered; she encourages us to forsake the urge to "control" and instead to savor the creativity characteristic of a classroom full of children with their brains turned on.

2

Pedagogy as pasta: The inexact art of teaching

Kelly Klinefelter Lee

ONE OF MY favorite Saturday afternoon reads is Marcella Hazan, the maven of classic Northern Italian cooking. Her food is delicious, her writing is straightforward and peppered with humor, and she is brutally honest about her vision of cooking. Honesty in a cookbook? You see, Marcella believes in enjoying the process of cooking and paying attention to every detail so that the result is authentic. This means decrying shortcuts, fussily choosing ingredients, and using careful judgment and observation rather than

NEW DIRECTIONS FOR SCHOOL LEADERSHIP, NO. 11, SPRING 1999 © JOSSEY-BASS PUBLISHERS

typical cookbook instructions of time and temperature. In short, she demands that her readers—her students of classic Italian cooking—immerse themselves, literally, in their cooking and pay no mind to the state of disorder on the kitchen counter.

She describes two methods of making pasta at home, one by electric machine, the other with one's hands and a manual roller. "Do not be tempted by one of those awful devices that masticate eggs and flour at one end and extrude a choice of pasta shapes through another end. What emerges is a mucilaginous and totally contemptible product," says Marcella of the former. But the instructions for making the pasta by hand and rolling it through the stainless steel contraption clamped to your kitchen counter go on for no less than five pages. And they are not easy instructions. They contain more words like "about" and "when you think" than do typical cookbook recipes. They require observation and judgment, as when she instructs you to knead the pasta dough for eight minutes and until it is "as smooth as baby skin."

Marcella is the genuine article of cooking. I love her. And I love her approach to cooking, for it is the same approach I aim to take as a teacher. I want my students to have a deep and rich understanding of ideas. We get there not by throwing together ingredients and automatically producing worksheets, quizzes, and multiple-choice tests, but by reading, discussing, working in groups, writing, relating the material to our own lives, asking moral questions, and exploring multiple perspectives.

This is messy teaching. It has clear goals and daily plans, but it allows for the imagination of the individual child and the unpredictability inherent in a room full of adolescents with their brains turned on. To do it well, one follows not a textbook of chapters and review questions but a map for understanding goals that are interrelated and complex and that offer points at which students can draw in their own life experiences. To sustain the energy and creativity it takes, this teacher needs professional camaraderie. Having excitement but no one with whom to share it is demoralizing. Having a dilemma but no one with whom to talk it through is frustrating. And it ultimately undermines the will to press ahead despite the challenges posed by this messy teaching.

I thought this student-centered teaching was the expectation at the Williams South Middle School in Chelsea, where I completed my first year of teaching. Maybe it really was. But I had a dreadfully difficult time doing these things at the Williams School and, in the end, I didn't feel like I was an authentic me at the school.

Isolation

The Williams School offered up lots of challenges for the first-year teacher. Chelsea is one of the poorest cities in the Commonwealth of Massachusetts and its schools show it. They were taken over by the state in the early 1990s when the town went bankrupt and are still run in cooperation with the Boston University School of Education. This relationship is, on the faculty level, rife with divisiveness and distrust.

The diversity of the students contributed to the chaos. Roughly one-third of my students spoke English as a second language. Many of the students had traumatic histories, having escaped from Latin America during the 1980s or most recently from Bosnia. They were unified by their refugee status, but that was all, sometimes, because they came from such vastly different classes and cultures. Even the kids who came from the same place were sometimes radically different: Consider a Bosnian gypsy who was never educated before the refugee camps, and a middle-class Bosnian girl who was accustomed to rising whenever the teacher entered the room.

Schools like those in Chelsea deal with so many issues—they are the social issues of the poor, whose impact on the classroom put me daily into a place of triage rather than teaching. In our cluster of sixty students, my coteacher and I discussed six cases of possible child abuse and neglect with the guidance office. About 10 percent of our students missed more than forty days of school. One child moved to an alternative school after assaulting a teacher and bringing a weapon to my class. Another threatened to bring a gun to school. And we met with a public health nurse who subsequently did a drop-in visit on a student who missed more than fifty days of school every year for the past three and is literate in neither English nor her family's native Spanish. When she was evaluated after eight years in this school system, we found that her IQ was 40.

I was ready for these aspects of teaching in Chelsea. I turned down a job in a middle-class suburb to teach in Chelsea; after teaching previously in Boston and Chicago public schools, I wanted these students. It was the response of the school to the students that was so difficult for me to digest.

The Williams School is one of those institutions really caught up in the tedium of institutionhood. It's an "I control therefore I am" kind of place. Instead of welcoming the children, nurturing their intellects and personalities, and appreciating their diversity of experience, it seeks to standardize them with rules and test scores. After student-teaching at the Fenway Middle College High School, a pilot school in Boston whose culture is built upon the individuality of its students, the Williams School was a shock.

The rules of the Williams School were not unlike those in an average American middle school, rural, urban, or otherwise. And I can't say any one of the rules was unreasonable. School is a place for socialization as well as education, and as the responsible adult, I believe in maintaining an environment of seriousness and respect.

There was a culture of unwritten rules at the Williams School, however, that required teachers to instill obedience in their students. Successful rule-keeping was silence. These rules were difficult for me to adhere to in my room. This is partly because I had a difficult time with classroom management. (I remember saying in my interview, "When the lessons are engaging, classroom management isn't much of a problem." There is a kernel of truth in this, but only a kernel.)

I also had difficulty with these unwritten rules, though, because of the way I taught. I'm talking about cooperative learning, discussion, and student-led projects, all of which were central to my daily lesson plans. These are great strategies. Many of my students benefited enormously from them. They made my authority and my classroom environment vulnerable, however, to the students who, accustomed to authoritarian rule in school, cannot behave appropriately when given responsibility for their own behavior. In the end, the time we wasted making transitions from group work to silent work to discussion was my responsibility. I was the teacher. But I was very challenged by the kids who took advantage of the opportunities that my methods gave.

As frustrated as I was with the wasted class time and poor student behavior, the hardest part was hearing via the grapevine what other teachers thought of me. The friendlier teachers reassured me by telling me that I got unlucky with a group of difficult kids assigned to my cluster. They knew my classroom wasn't like the others in the building, but they liked me and wanted it not to be my fault. Other teachers were not so kind. I do not know the specifics of their comments; the person who told me that they had been speaking ill of the behavior of my students and my ineptitude was nice enough to spare me the details.

So as much as I believed in my methods, I felt like a failure because I could not do what was truly valued at the Williams School: make my students obey my commands. I took comfort in my belief that the aim of a school is to enforce the skills and passions of learning and that that aim is only achieved in an environment of creative expression and intellectual curiosity. Control and power and humiliating disciplinary procedures undermine learning, I told myself. Sitting silently for fifty minutes at a time completing fill-in-the-blank worksheets does not inspire understanding; discussing and debating and cooperating inspire understanding. But I got tired of standing out in the crowd.

Getting noticed, you see, is not the objective at the Williams Middle School. I inferred this message from my fellow teachers: If they don't hear about you from other teachers, if you don't go to them with too many problems, if they don't really know what's going on in your classroom, then they can't have any reason to get rid of you. Anonymity, in other words, was viewed as the route to job security. I should have known that from the moment my unofficial mentor told me that I was joining a wonderful faculty, one in

which "no one tries to do anything creative or be better than anyone else." The message was driven home after a faculty discussion
with Edwin DeLattre, dean of the Boston University School of
Education. Only two of us teachers spoke during the hour-long
meeting. Several of those who were there and didn't speak com-
mented to me afterwards that I was brave to raise my hand and
open my mouth. "I don't want them to know my name," one of my
colleagues said.

The truth is, as much as I disagreed with Dean DeLattre's philosophy in that discussion, I loved the opportunity to talk about
education. In fact, I was thrilled driving home that day. That simple conversation was the first philosophical discussion I had ever
had with adults within the four walls of the Williams School since
my job interview.

As it turned out, this isolation from my fellow teachers had a
greater impact on me than any other aspect of my school's culture.

Teaching for me is like cooking is for Marcella. It is a spiritual
journey. I want to enjoy the messiness of the classroom. I need to
love my students, tell them that I love them, and bring together
their often disparate qualities and experiences in a process of learning that requires constant judgment and adaptability. Being a good
teacher is not about following a recipe. Being a good teacher is
about intellect and understanding, passion, empathy, patience, and
dogged optimism. And it's also highly imprecise, just like making
pasta by hand. The critical elements of teaching are creativity,
thoughtfulness, problem solving, careful observation, and instinct.

And because teaching is like this for me, the culture of the
Williams School simply exhausted my spirit. We didn't talk about
teaching and learning. Our faculty meetings were quick exchanges
of rules and guidelines; a colleague who consistently raised her
hand with questions of substance was branded a "borderline insub-
ordinate" by one and accused of "wasting our time" by another.

I felt like there was no one to turn to in the building to talk
about teaching and learning. I even felt isolated from my friends
who taught in other school districts. They asked about Chelsea. I
told them ad nauseam about my kids (and their problems and my

duties around those problems). They said things like, "Yeah, my students in Brookline have so many problems, too. Kids everywhere have problems." And they were right, because adolescence is so damn tough. They were wrong, too, because there are differences between Brookline and Chelsea. Compare poor and middle-class school systems and see where graduation and higher education rates and test scores are lowest. I fell into that bitter inner-city teacher trap, almost thriving on the adversity. With perspective gained I will say this: Kids everywhere have problems, but the crisis is simply greater in some places than in others.

In short, it was a lonely time.

Trying and failing

I honestly feel that my loneliness kept me from making any great impact upon the institution. I tried. This is an excerpt from my journal, written in January.

I approached my principal yesterday morning in the lobby of our middle school. As students milled about us, anxious for their free breakfasts and a chance to socialize with their friends, I asked the principal excitedly about the possibility of starting a mentorship program. "I want to pull ten or twelve leaders—strong personalities, I mean, not the honor roll kids, necessarily—from my class list for next year and run a summer program with them. You know, run them through a ropes course, get them ready to be on board with our philosophy of education, ready to be positive leaders in the classroom."

"And I want lots of money," I continued. "It has to be off-site, out of school, not institutional at all. Catered food. Luxurious. First class treatment, to make them feel special. To get them invested. Three or four days," I said, "of intense preparation and dialogue."

The principal loved the idea, although I noticed that "aren't you an idealistic first-year teacher" grin peeking through. And then he said to me words that have been ringing chaotically in my head ever since. "Isn't it nice to talk about education once in a while, Kelly?"

This was, indeed, the first time Steve and I talked about education, about pedagogy and philosophy and strategy, since my interview in August.

In the end this program didn't materialize. The principal told me, when I asked, that no, it wasn't going to work out. He mentioned the central office, how busy things are, you know how it goes. It didn't matter that I had suggested the program. None of my colleagues knew about my ideas; there wasn't really a venue for sharing such things.

When I graduated from the Teaching and Curriculum Program at Harvard, I felt that my mission and that of my fellow students was to go out and be agents of change in the schools. As I talked to my fellow first-year teachers, I was astounded by the things they accomplished and couldn't help but compare myself with them. I didn't fare well by comparison.

I make myself feel better about my mediocrity by saying I accomplished a little something here and there. I brought affection into the school lives of my students, affection that many very desperately need. I was an adult who had high expectations for all of them. As session after session of cooperative learning activities fell victim to poor behavior, I persevered, telling them that I knew they could do it. It got better with time; my resolve had had an impact on them. I invited them to bring their lives into the classroom, especially through writing. They loved the journal entries in which they had to imagine themselves in a historical situation and describe their feelings and responses.

There were some truly beautiful moments as a result, like the time we were talking about the lives of women in New Spain and a boy who was rarely engaged in class work said, "Ms. Klinefelter, I don't understand why people wouldn't want women to work," and a lively two-hour discussion ensued. Nearly every student raised a hand that day! There was the time I assigned the kids in groups to write their own bill of rights. I paused for a moment between visits to the cooperative learning groups and gazed upon thirty students engaged and participating. Every group independently included education as an important right. They were indignant when I told them that there is no right to education in our Bill of Rights. When we did a unit on writing research papers, the students chose their own topics. It gave a young survivor of rape the chance to explore the life of Maya Angelou; the depth of meaning for her was greater than I could gauge. My students and I cried at the end of a favorite novel and sat silently for five minutes, blown away by our emotion. (This kind of quiet was unheard of in my room.) And we loved language together, especially when we read, acted out, and drew our way through very difficult poems, including Coleridge's "Kubla Khan." As a learning community, my classes and I never fully achieved our goals, but they were high and they were clear. That's something.

Did I affect my school besides making the third floor a little louder than the others? If school reform is for the sake of students, not institutions, then maybe I did.

Questions for the future

I am not teaching this year; my infant daughter has beckoned me home. I can hardly wait to start anew another September. But I am left with several decisions.

Will I teach where I feel I can make a profound difference by trying to change an institution like the Williams School? I suspect I would feel like a traitor if I didn't teach where there was a need for change, because I come to this profession with my politics, social philosophy, and religious faith all requiring me to give where most is needed. At the same time, though, I fear losing sight of what I really love, which is the classroom, for the immediate challenges posed by the committees and meetings that accompany school change. Selfishly, I want to spend my energy serving the students directly. It's what I am good at. It's what I love.

Am I capable of overcoming the isolation and doing my best work in such a spiritually and intellectually depleted setting? I could work on my resolve and seek out camaraderie outside of my school. And many people find their intellectual stimulation entirely outside of work. But at what personal cost would I do this? I felt last year like my job was punishment for naive idealism, and it made me feel in some strange construction superior to my colleagues, which in turn made me sick with disgust at myself. Perhaps it is unfair to myself and my family to step into a trap of self-flagellation and despair again.

The real question is this: Which parts of myself and my values would I sacrifice by teaching in a school that likes the neat, clean, predictable educational models that are efficient but, like Marcella's electric pasta machine, produce a pale version of what education can and should be?

KELLY KLINEFELTER LEE *is presently enjoying a hiatus from teaching to attend to the needs of Eleanor, her newborn daughter and primary beneficiary of Marcella Hazan's technique. During the 1997–1998 school year, Kelly taught seventh-grade English and social studies at the Williams South Middle School in Chelsea, Massachusetts. Prior to that, Kelly attended the Harvard Graduate School of Education and the University of Chicago and spent three years working at Facing History and Ourselves.*

While noble, pledging to change the world in one's first year of teaching is naive. Logistical pressures dominate the work of first-year teachers and restrict their impact on the larger school community. Nevertheless, over the course of the year Brian plowed forward, attempting to make a difference where he could. Ultimately, he came to understand that change must first occur at the microlevel, in the classroom, before it can happen at the macrolevel, schoolwide. Although simple, Brian's lesson presents a challenge that all well-meaning pedagogues encounter.

3

Teaching with care

Brian Poon

SITTING IN THAT dilapidated classroom, interviewing for my dream job, I was more nervous than I can effectively describe. The sounds of walls crumbling beneath the weight of a wrecking ball echoed through the room, reminding all that Brookline High School was in the midst of a $40 million renovation. Over the next five years the building had to absorb a boom in population from 1,700 to 2,200 students and move its technology into the twenty-first century. The kids represented an incredible montage of backgrounds and, according to the reputation, had forged a progressive community with an enlightened and engaged faculty. The instruction

NEW DIRECTIONS FOR SCHOOL LEADERSHIP, NO. 11, SPRING 1999 © JOSSEY-BASS PUBLISHERS

at Brookline High was excellent by all state standards, from test scores to graduation rates. For me, becoming a teacher was about the struggle against apathy and the promotion of an ethic of care that taught students that they mattered. I longed to bring my ardor for teaching young people to think for themselves to a school that celebrated similar ideas. In short: I wanted to work at Brookline High School.

Enveloped in a conversation that would determine my professional future, I spoke with a social studies teacher and the department chair about the necessity of educating students' hearts as well as their minds. The two men pushed the conversation beyond pleasantries about diversity and practice, forcing me to confront fundamental issues of balancing content with skills, compassion with responsibility. Committing the interviewee's cardinal sin, I was honest: Although I wasn't the best classroom manager and I needed to develop my teaching techniques, I was passionate about students and teaching. The two men apparently appreciated my philosophy: in September I found myself working at Brookline High School.

As I approached teaching at Brookline, I was ebullient. I was also scared. I met with social studies teachers before school began to talk about my classes and the school, but nothing prepared me for teaching full time. With my idealism in tow, I spent the first month attempting to create communities out of my classes and to change the world. Central to teaching was the idea that I could excite my young charges to take action and influence the world. If I could give responsibility to my kids then they would go out from my classroom and act responsibly. My initial dialogues about classroom rules with my kids were well intentioned, but often devolved into, "taking advantage of the new teacher" time. Although I was saying, "What do you think is a fair tardy system?" what I was teaching was, "I am not in control of this situation." During those first weeks, it was hard.

Despite my initial rough start, I rejected the mantra, "Don't smile until November." I tried to be a real person to my kids while retaining professional distance. With long hair and untucked shirts, I knew that I was different. I was determined not to objectify my students. Walking through the school, I spoke with my students about nonacademic subjects as well as what we had just read in class. "How's hoops going Kevin? I student-taught at North. So I know about half of their team. Have you done your homework?" A Harvard-trained pedagogue, I practiced teaching for understanding. I had read Freire. I wanted dialogical learning, conversations that mattered. But it was hard. Praxis is much easier to say than to practice. My kids knew that I was young. They took advantage of me at times—but I also think that I earned their respect by being consistent and resilient.

I often pretended to myself that it wasn't all that difficult and somehow I had avoided the first-year teacher disease. By November, however, I was fully aware that I was physically and mentally exhausted. Swamped with papers to grade and unruly classes to control, I battled daily to keep my head above water. Whenever I was confused or depressed about the conundrums that invariably confounded me, however, my colleagues, my friends, buttressed me with an incredible amount of emotional and curricular support. Collaborative teaching wasn't the norm, but for both my philosophy and world history classes I had fantastic colleagues with whom I shared lesson plans and resources.

Bolstered by this help, I plugged along and hoped that in my own little classroom I could do my thing and effect change there. Doing my own thing, however, has never really been my thing, so I looked to the school community for opportunities to get more involved.

My first chance came from the lunchroom. The Cafe, as it was called, provided a tragic metaphor for the privilege and waste of Brookline. At the end of lunch half-eaten pieces of food and sullied paper products littered the room. The teachers then patrolled the Cafe and encouraged kids to throw their trash away. Often teachers, not students, picked up the Styrofoam trays covered with coagulated cheese and deposited them in the bins. Our efforts were to no avail, because at the end of each lunch period the abandoned room would be a disgrace left to the custodians.

Disgusted, I decided I would go through the proper channels and motivate the kids to help clean up. I e-mailed the headmaster and got the go ahead to try to change things. Hesitant to infringe on anyone's space, I spoke to the maintenance people about the feasibility of a clean Cafe movement. They doubted my potential effectiveness but consented to anything I wanted to try.

I attempted to rally my homeroom around a Change the Culture of the School Club that would not only make a difference, but would also earn them service credit toward graduation. My idea was to get the students invested in creating a better environment. Maybe their example would lead to change. About half of my class agreed to meet me on Monday at lunch to plan our strategy for cleaning up, but come Monday I sat alone waiting. No one except my wonderful co-homeroom teacher arrived. This led to a fruitful conversation about why kids don't show up. She told me that it was intrinsic to the school's identity that everyone was so busy with his or her sport, activity, or work that initiatives fell to the wayside. It was easier to be submerged in your own world than to think of the school as a whole. The next week I attempted to rally the troops again, but I had gotten so caught up in the day-to-day that I forgot our meeting time. No one missed me.

Brookline is big, and its size can be intimidating. It is large enough that a student or a teacher could almost disappear. Due to the organization, the school is greatly divided and there isn't much communication among the constituent parts. Each department works independently on projects and policies, a situation that leads to in-fighting for resources. English teachers have four classes. Science and math have special lab blocks. Social studies has five classes and a greater student load. Jealous of what other departments had and hoarding our own departmental advantages, we didn't work very well together as a school.

Despite the disaggregate nature of the school we did meet fairly frequently. The faculty, staff, and administration met informally over coffee and donuts every Friday. There were also departmental and faculty meetings on a semiregular basis. These gatherings, however, tended to be unproductive. There were so many issues festering that when we sat down to discuss, we vented anger rather than planned action. The feeling I got when I left our meetings was that although there were some valid criticisms raised, nothing would be done; things would remain the same. Although I had good intentions and was quite motivated, the culture of apathy was entrenched, and I succumbed. There were too many papers to grade and lessons to plan. As I succumbed, I felt my frustration grow.

Systemic issues of large organizations were not the only problem. Students' apparent lack of care and general disrespect spoke to our school's deeper issues. It wasn't just the trash in the cafeteria, but the blatant rudeness some students had for their teachers and each other. In general, Brookline High School is a model of decency. The kids that go to our school tend to be good kids; the students are kind to their teachers and their teachers are kind to them. But the profanity shouted in the halls, the sad truth that girls get shoved into lockers for being in the wrong place, the dearth of personal responsibility that students demonstrated as they disregarded basic high school rules of which they were well aware—all of it depressed the hell out of me. Certainly students decided for themselves how they wanted to behave, but teachers had a role in modeling and shaping behavior.

If teachers imagine that teaching only happens within the confines of their classroom, the learning for students will never extend beyond their fifty-minute block. School is one of the few places where young people not only can be socialized with societal norms of right and wrong, but also learn to think independently. The point of rules should never be just to get kids to do what you want. Rather, everyone needs to learn how to live cooperatively within a group. The concept that actions have ramifications is elusive in our culture. People must be taught causality. The issues of eating in the halls, listening to walkmen, and smoking next to the school were not that important to me, but they were against the rules of the school. We knew that the students' behavior was wrong but we failed to react consistently. We watched it happen. I watched.

Teachers have the autonomy to make amazing classes, but this also means that teachers are often left all alone. It is easy to become isolated. The school culture that sanctified the autonomy of the classroom also made me feel weak if I asked for help. When I closed the door of my room, there was this sense of excitement that I could do anything. There was also, however, the lingering sense of danger that anything could happen. I never saw any other teacher in the school, let alone my department, teach. Every day at lunch I would sit down with some of the most brilliant pedagogues in the country, teachers who produced an abundance of fours and fives in our advanced-placement classes and cultivated deep seriousness of purpose in our lower tracked classes. Even though I was invited to watch, I never encroached on another teacher's demesnes. It felt intrusive. I constructed a fortress around my room and the culture of the school seemed to reinforce my walls.

There is a myth of the great Brookline Teacher who is so amazingly brilliant that he can do anything without any help. Classroom management and curriculum development are nonissues because we are so smart. In my imagination, because I had planned my world history classes so well, the last two blocks of the day should go smoothly. So on that Friday late in May, when the sun had cooked the class to 105 degrees and there was no shade blocking the glare, and I couldn't contain my students, I felt like a horrible teacher.

Victims of our own prestige, we often fight the good fight, on our own, without seeking support. I was a hotshot new teacher—I didn't need help. But I did, and I was afraid to ask. When we finally do ask, there is a degree of shame. Either things have gotten so crazy that we should never have let them get this far along, or the problem that we observe is so banal that to mention it is to whine. As a first-year teacher there are many understanding nods, and often there is sound advice. But when you are stuck behind a pile of philosophy journals and your F block thinks that it is fun to torture the different kid, words do not assuage one's despair. To invite the department chair into my room or call in a dean was tantamount to admitting defeat. I didn't want to be perceived as a quitter; I was worthy to work at Brookline High.

Finally, the administration did come to my aid in an extreme case and my department chair was supportive when I was at my wits' end. In one of my classes a student made disparaging remarks and gestures during a conversation about heterosexist discrimination. After confronting him and asking him to stop he told me that no one was going to tell him what to do. He informed me that his faux lisp and the flip of his wrist had been misunderstood. I called in my department chair and the student's dean. At those moments, however, I felt defeated and naive. Why couldn't I have dealt with this problem? Support at that point often feels like an affirmation of your failure as a teacher. My colleagues consistently advised me on students or pedagogy, but they too suffered from the sense of failure that comes from asking for help.

Part of the problem came from the fact that Brookline appeared to do everything right. When I interviewed with the headmaster, he showed me the letterhead for the school stationery. It read, The High School. We were the platonic form High School to which all other schools were but essences. Despite our hubris, we did many important things very well. There was not a group that was not celebrated, a day that was not acknowledged, an initiative that was not funded that supported community mores and celebrated difference. The greatness of Brookline, however, was assumed. We took it for granted. Parents wanted accountability for student behavior but only so long as it was not at the expense of their child. The teachers were tired.

Despite the initiatives of the school, the hard conversations about individual responsibility and group culpability failed to materialize. We didn't have a cohesive vision, and this created a tension between our ideals and our reality. Due to our faculty diaspora, or perhaps our entrenched practices, there was no coordinated effort to bring the lessons of responsibility into our curriculum. After the Gay/Straight/Lesbian Day of assemblies, there was no time to debrief the powerful experiences. There was little time to complete our own curricula, and with state-mandated testing, there was even less time. By assuming our own greatness, we were blind to problems that ravaged the school.

Our students were the most disrespectful fans I have ever encountered. At basketball games some students were abominable.

Once at a game a boy wouldn't stop yelling at the opposing team's center because she was apparently too tall. This switched to calling his friends faggots as they walked by. At this point I turned around and told him that this behavior was not permissible. He responded that the other student was his friend so it was fine. During another basketball game, the crowd chanted "Buckwheat! Buckwheat!" at a black player from a rival school. When the athletic director attempted to bring some civility to the crowd by removing the worst perpetrators, he was cursed at by some students. They could perceive only how their rights had been infringed upon and not that they were at all responsible.

Our headmaster spoke out strongly against disrespectful behavior at athletic contests and indeed our sporting events became more civil, but the deeper issues of what caused the kids to act with such disregard went unchecked. This made my heart break. What were we teaching kids and what were they learning if they thought that our enraged reactions to blatant racism and disrespect were merely overreaction and misinterpretation?

At the end of the year, our seniors were told in no uncertain terms if they were caught with alcohol at the Prom or the After-Prom Party, they would not be allowed to walk at graduation. That evening a bunch of my teacher friends and I had dinner before we chaperoned the dance. The topic of discussion was the waning respect of students for authority. But more important, we bemoaned the loss of their self-respect. We craved accountability but we feared Draconian backlash.

Later that night, a large group of students arrived at the dance in a rented bus. Our headmaster and security were tipped off that there was alcohol on the bus. Upon entering the bus, they saw bottles strewn everywhere. When the students returned to the bus they were confronted. Once again, students vilified adults. Their rights had been infringed. No mention was made of the fact that they could have been arrested or worse, hurt. Parents railed against the headmaster for his audacity. The faculty fully supported our headmaster, but we were all in shock. What had we taught if these were the lessons that our most mature students learned?

I, like many of my colleagues, retreated to what I thought I could control. I attempted to create a classroom where we made time to talk about issues. My classes had students of widely heterogeneous backgrounds and ability. I don't think it was exceptional in that my students, despite their differences, got along. I made sure, however, that we had the tough conversations. Sometimes it exhausted my kids because they didn't want to talk about how Calvinism in the Protestant Reformation led to the rigidity of Puritan Massachusetts. How our nation's ethos was framed by those who thought that those who were successful were good and going to heaven and those who were not white, Anglo-Saxon Protestant deserved hell was a tough topic for a group of kids—especially since many of them were the ones condemned to the netherworld. It was easier if philosophy class wasn't personal and kids could think about theory rather than confront their own choices. The gap between the theories we espoused to believe in and the way we lived was central to the class, however, and we were all challenged to live our own beliefs. It is one thing to comprehend how Plato divided the Republic; it is another to evaluate how that theoretical society mirrored our own and whether or not that was good. In my class on gender in society it wasn't enough to just read about how roles are constructed, students had to go into society and break norms to see how the other is constructed. One of my male students was chased out of a nail salon for requesting a manicure. A female student was laughed at for ordering the steak and potatoes while her male companion asked for the salad with the low-fat dressing on the side. My classroom was always a place where the personal was political and the abstractions of book learning were steeped in the reality of everyday life.

What perhaps was more important, I made time for my kids on a personal level. The school just seemed too big to effect large-scale change, but I tried to model love and care for every one of my students. It was exhausting, but vital. So I stayed after school with kids terrified about next year. I got some phone calls at home from students who were scared of their father. I had long talks on the sidelines of basketball games with kids who had lost hope. That all seemed part of the price of loving my kids. After class I heard from seniors about the rampant drug abuse and drinking, as well as the shocking number of abortions of which nothing was otherwise ever spoken. Most of the time, however, modeling care had to do with going to hockey games, dance performances, and saying "What's up?" in the halls. I read a slew of college essays and wrote a fair number of recommendations. Personal connection was what it was all about. Students needed to be affirmed individuals, not anonymous faces in the crowd.

For me, perhaps my greatest impact on the institution came almost by mistake. I fell into restarting and running the mock trial team. There had been a mock trial team at Brookline five years earlier, but it had died out. A friend from graduate school who had been a lawyer and had assisted in mock trial at his student-teaching school inquired whether there was interest at Brookline for starting up a team. The old coordinator was willing to restart the team, but as the time for the tournament drew near he was unable to get involved. I found myself as the teacher coach of a Brookline mock trial team that had been promised, but did not exist. While putting up signs about being a warrior lawyer, I was almost scared to see who would show up for our meeting. I am not sure how this motley collection of young people came to symbolize hope, but they became a vital way for me to make a difference.

It was a random group. Often, members of the team would look around the room and laugh because they knew that without mock trial there would be no way that they would be standing in the same room together. At the outset they were awful. After our first full practice, my friend and lawyer coach turned to me and just grimaced. Despite how terrible we were, there was faith. It was important. Mock trial became an odd representation of love and dedication. Every Sunday and some Saturdays we would get together and work. Differences were understood and appreciated. I don't imagine that it was my inspired leadership and it certainly wasn't my mastery of trial law that brought the team together, but as a group of diverse folk we actively listened and supported one another. The students had a sense of ownership of the team.

If we were going to be competitive, then everyone had to matter and everyone had to pull his or her weight. One of our witnesses for the trial was having personal problems, so another student who had recently immigrated to this country needed to take his place. As we practiced direct and cross examinations, it was clear that he was having a tough time understanding the language. So we drilled and practiced and hammered out responses until we were all exhausted. When our trial against Charlestown High came around, our witness was brilliant. He nailed the direct examination and during the cross examination, he stuck it to the opposing team's lawyer. His success was our success. Trials were stressful and the competition was fierce, but we pulled together and won. When we were knocked out of play-off contention, it was amazing how hard we took it. One of the Russian girls on the team said, through tears, that she had never meant to care so much about a Brookline activity, but she loved mock trial.

It's hard to describe, but the members of the mock trial team infused me with hope. In so many ways they were an example of what I wanted my teaching experience to be like: diverse folk learning from one another and taking a vested interest in their vital role in a community. We were both individually and collectively responsible for our success and failure. I certainly didn't want teaching to be a litigious, competitive squabble before a judge, but I did want to bring together people to effect change. I learned that by affecting the world on the microlevel that you affect the world on the macrolevel. Maybe I didn't change the big picture at BHS, but I could carve out a piece and work with it.

I ended my first year of teaching utterly exhausted but hopeful. It occurred to me that of course the problem was too big to do alone. Young people everywhere are facing the onslaught of a media-driven culture that assaults them with images of apathy. There are real differences that divide people for a reason, but there are also real reasons to bring different people together. Although I found myself small and intimidated before the hugeness of the struggle to make education and life choices matter, it was the right struggle.

In my class, in the hallway, at my home, I changed the institution by modeling care. Of course Brookline was too large for the lone avenger. But I wasn't alone. Teachers and administrators throughout the school felt that Brookline needed to change. But we had to work together. Shifting the ethos of a proud institution in a proud community is arduous work. Learning to work together is not easy; however, it is not labor in vain. Rather, it is the most vital work around.

BRIAN POON *is presently teaching philosophy, gender studies, and world history at Brookline High School in Brookline, Massachusetts. Before beginning his Sisyphean offensive against Brookline's cafeteria in the fall of 1997, Brian attended the Harvard Graduate School of Education. Prior to graduate school, he served as assistant director of admission for three years at his alma mater, Haverford College.*

*In wealthy suburbs across the nation, students fol-
low a well-trod path to success. They enroll in every
advanced placement course offered, score well on the
SATs, participate in a host of extracurricular activities, and gain admission to the most selective colleges. But what do they actually learn? As a product
of such an environment, Allyson discovered that
teaching students to think required much more
than this traditional model. While questioning her
students, Allyson learned that a teacher, particularly one who has excelled in the conventional sense
of that term, must question herself.*

4

Teaching to question

Allyson Mizoguchi

ENTERING THE TEACHING profession did not begin as a crusade to
find my voice, although that is what it has become. I had little idea
that I grew up essentially voiceless within the confines of a conventional education and a sheltered community. Once I began to
teach, however, I began a revelatory, and sometimes painful,
process of altering my understanding of what a true education can
be. I realized that I neither wholly received one nor am entirely
certain how to ensure one for my students.

Growing up in a small suburb of San Diego, I was a good English student and a good history student—but rarely a student of

NEW DIRECTIONS FOR SCHOOL LEADERSHIP, NO. 11, SPRING 1999 © JOSSEY-BASS PUBLISHERS

learning or of life. Although there were many activities for a student to try in elementary school and junior high—band, art, music, dance, woodshop—by the time I reached high school, the opportunities and the encouragement dwindled. Art and music programs were the first to be cut from our high school district because of budget constraints; all practical arts such as shop and cooking were cut next. The definition of success became narrower. It was as though the many different, swirling paths we were allowed to take as youngsters all led to one superhighway of achievement that effectively paved over other routes.

Like many of my peers, I became good at meeting expectations by using the formulas and paradigms I was fed. True success revolved around high grades, stunning extracurricular achievements, and the ability to pull it all off with a healthy social life. The older my classmates and I became, the less tolerated and less nurtured other forms and levels of achievement seemed to be.

I found success through obedience. I was rewarded for having answers rather than questions. I did not question because I did not know how to question. With few exceptions, I did not often reach, dare, or even grow personally and intellectually. I was able to memorize and drill my way to a competitive GPA; I followed directions carefully and did the work. I was on the superhighway without knowing that there were other roads, other objectives to an education besides grades, standardized tests, and college admissions. Once I was on the superhighway, I lost peripheral vision.

From high school, I predictably entered college, and then predictably entered graduate school. But there, the superhighway ended. As part of my teacher preparation, I was asked to reflect on my own years of being a student. Gradually, I began to realize that my achievements rested largely on the shoulders of those who had come before me. By the time I graduated from high school, very few accomplishments were entirely my own. They had all been thought before, done before. Somewhere, muddled in the lessons and beliefs of my teachers, were my thoughts. To be an effective teacher, I needed to unearth those thoughts, find my voice, and learn how to value it. It wasn't until I became a teacher that I discovered how to be a learner.

Walking onto Wayland High School's campus for the first time as an English teacher, I immediately felt at home. It is much like the high school I attended, both inside and out. Its suburban location, motivated students, and extensive resources contribute to its strong reputation in the region. It is the sort of community to which families move solely for the schools. Although relatively small (700 students), the high school is preparing itself for inevitable growth in the next few years. I was part of the largest rush of new teachers in the school's history. When I arrived, I noticed a real gap—of pedagogy and experience—between the veterans in their forties and fifties and the much younger rookies. The veterans in the school are mostly exhilarated by the "new blood" in the school, although I detect some tension and skepticism of the new teachers. Maintaining the high academic standards typical of Wayland is a task some veterans doubt we can fulfill. We bring vigor and youth (and inexperience and risk) into a school that has historically been quite traditional. Wayland prides itself on being progressive in providing multicultural and antiracist education, a torch that only a handful of the veterans, and the majority of the rookies, bear.

I faced Wayland's academic standards with some degree of trepidation born out of inexperience and an aching recognition. I lacked overall confidence and was unsure that I could maintain the tradition of academic excellence. I was also easily able to view that tradition from the inside: I know what it is like to be a student in such a school because I was one. I quickly understood the subtleties of the school—which students would be my friends if I were a student at Wayland, the hierarchy of cliques, the power that parents and the community have, the dangerous mix of affluence and high expectations. At first eager to contribute to a preexisting set of high standards, I felt that I instantly had a curricular template from which to work. However, being on the other side of the student-teacher equation for the first time gave me a perspective that would eventually change much more than my pedagogic approaches to teaching. I suddenly felt that I was behind the scenes of a play I had participated in for much of my entire life, the drama of "small, competitive suburban school." Amid the academic accolades and Harvard-bound graduates, I saw that Wayland tends to produce the type of learner that I had been: a voiceless learner, a student with many answers but few questions, the master of conformity. Although I recognized these students, I did not see myself in them at first. I only pitied them.

I give credit to my honors sophomore class for first nudging my consciousness. In contrast to my college preparatory freshmen, the lower of the two tracks, my sophomores were constantly concerned with their grades. Besides keeping track of every point they scored, they had no qualms about challenging my grading procedures. I often heard, "How much is this worth?" and "Why did I lose points on this?" During group work in class, I would hear, "Is this going to be graded?" Worse, during class discussions, when I used the chalkboard, students would inevitably ask, "Do we need to write this down?" Why can't an honors student decide what is and what isn't important? Why can't an honors student ask insightful questions and issue interesting challenges that pertain to the topic at hand, rather than questions regarding procedure, grading, and logistics?

It was maddening. Attempting to introduce new materials to the supposedly highest-achieving students was to become a chore. As students argued with me about the grades I had given them, I felt instantly defensive and angry. "But forget about the grade," I heard myself tell one student. "What did you learn?" Her response: "I don't know." Then I have failed you as your teacher, I wanted to tell her. I felt as though I had been kicked in the stomach.

My tirades against their obsessive grade-grubbing sounded hollow. The students weren't going to budge. "Then how will we get into college?" was their reply to my reprimands. The sad truth is, they won't get into college without high grades and stellar extracurricular activities (and hence sleepless nights and ridiculous arguments about grades they received). As long as teachers and students perpetuate this construction of success, I can't fight against it. The system is larger, much larger, than we are.

Attacking the conflict from a different direction, I did away with multiple choice tests, fill-in-the-blank quizzes, and vocabulary exams. I experimented with rubrics and portfolios, brought crayons and markers to class for presentations, and arranged the desks in countless different configurations. The students were spinning as fast I was. But colored paper and music in the lesson plans did not remedy the core of the conflict. The solution did not lie in the structural approaches to my lessons, but in the objectives behind them and the questions they raised. My students, I realized, did not know how to learn—and, I slowly admitted to myself, I did not know how to teach them how to learn.

I have a vision of what students should be like: constantly craving information, relentlessly questioning and challenging, energetic and bright, and eager. Grades, standardized achievement, are not part of this vision. But I was never this student; I was the archetypal student within the system. I had been that shallow learner. I was attempting to teach my students to learn, when I had never truly known how to learn. I would need to learn how to learn, how to question, and how to help my students find their voices as I retrieved my own. I needed not to be the voiceless teacher creating voiceless students. I wanted to nurture a different kind of learner, the kind I wish I had been.

I began again. If the core of learning is questioning, then my students need to be able to question my purposes in each lesson, my objectives behind each assignment. They need to own what they learn. Being questioned outright by my students, however, threatened the confidence I wanted in a classroom of students not much younger than I. Were my interpretations of the literature valid? Were they profound enough to share with my students? Would I be thoroughly discredited if they disagreed? In the middle of flipping and floundering through the reformulated curriculum, I had a pivotal conversation with one of my mentor teachers. "Your job is not to have the answers," she told me. "Your job is to teach them to question." But without answers, what would I teach?

Like a domesticated animal, I was too used to being safe; I was too used to hiding my own thoughts—my voice—behind the rhetoric of people who had already written down or lectured about those ideas. My fear of being questioned, of not having "the answer," made me realize that it had not been for lack of imagination that I did not question in high school. It was lack of courage. It would be daring for me to consider other angles as a teacher, be willing to be challenged and to change, yet I saw no other way to subvert the system around us.

Encouraging my students to question me is both frightening and freeing for me. I am made uncomfortable by posing provocative statements, debating issues, and leaving discussions unfinished. In attempting to nurture my students' voices, I am inadvertently freeing my own. I am avenging the countless hours I spent in high school classrooms, passively absorbing information. In discussions with my students about literary theory, classism, the power of language, I hear a new voice coming from inside. I have volume, passion, and opinions. I have discovered that I can be an *advocate*, a *debater*, a *negotiator*, and a *mediator*, all words that characterize the role of *teacher*, and words I never before would have used to describe myself.

I still see myself in the voiceless students at Wayland. It seems that we are all, students and teachers, powerless against our frequently single-minded purposes: SATs, grades, college, multiple-choice exams. When I see my students flip to the grade on an essay and then throw the rest away into the garbage—that is voicelessness; when my students ache for someone to "just tell us the answer!"—that is voicelessness.

I believe that the students have too little influence on a system that bears down on them. Likewise, I feel stifled by a societal perception of what learning and academic success means, the very perception of which I am a product. It seems impossible to change an entire learning trend, in which the fruits of an education are stamped on a transcript rather than found in enlightening conversation or in a letter to a friend. Beyond the daily frustrations of being a teacher, the monumental task of altering the perceptions around me is chilling.

Shall my voice eventually be heard beyond the four walls of my classroom? In the department head's office when I want to change the curriculum, in the superintendent's office when we need more money, in the governor's ears when I want systemic change? How loudly, how far, should my voice carry?

While my colleagues from education school talk of educational reform, starting charter schools, and writing grant proposals, I am busy with self-discovery in my own classroom. This type of change is truly change from within; by changing my own perceptions first, I hope to alter those individuals—students, teachers, and administrators—around me. Change imposed from the outside makes little sense to me. I need to tackle the changes that I feel inside. I admit that teaching has become, to a certain degree, a selfish venture, self-serving in its pursuit. I have gained more knowledge, more understanding, and more courage, not to mention a yearly love affair with almost 100 students. Yet by redefining myself as a learner first and a teacher second, perhaps I can reach those virtually silent students whom I recognize so well.

ALLYSON MIZOGUCHI *teaches ninth- and tenth-grade English at Wayland High School in Wayland, Massachusetts. In her free time, Allyson coaches the Wayland Warriors JV girls' soccer team. Allyson graduated from Stanford University in 1995, worked in San Diego area schools for one year, and then attended Harvard Graduate School of Education.*

Engaged teaching necessarily becomes a deeply personal endeavor. Though it presents many challenges, the relationship between teacher and student remains the focal point of schools. Buttressed by institutional support, a teacher can blend the emotional and intellectual development of a student. Marco's challenges to integrate the personal and professional exhausted him but convinced him of the overall necessity of this enterprise.

5

Vulnerable relationships: Connections between family and teaching

Marco Curnen

LAST NIGHT I SAT in the kitchen, alone, in an apartment that had grown quiet as all the other members of my family had retreated to their bedrooms in preparation for the night's rest. It struck me how unfamiliar this scene had become for me over the course of the summer, when I did not feel compelled to prepare for teaching on a regular basis. Most often, I am upstairs reading or joking around, saying "good night" with my partner, my daughter, and my son. On this night, however, I decided to take some time to reflect in my journal, to write down some thoughts about the upcoming academic year. I wondered how often during the next nine months

NEW DIRECTIONS FOR SCHOOL LEADERSHIP, NO. 11, SPRING 1999 © JOSSEY-BASS PUBLISHERS

I would be spending this kind of time, late at night, preparing for the following day.

In addition to being a wonderful time to recharge one's "batteries," summer is an intensely therapeutic time for me. Whereas during the year, the restraints of the daily schedule mean I cannot spend as much time with my children, the summer opens up the schedule again. In particular, with my two-year-old son, the summer has allowed for a bond to flourish between us that inspires me to give thanks for life on a daily basis. The summer also gives me the flexibility and recovery time to exercise on a more regular basis than I seem to be able to achieve during the school year. I share these examples only because I find them relevant as I return to year number two at Brookline High with a healthier, more balanced perspective than I remember having last year at this time.

As a new teacher, everything was new! I didn't know where to go, what to hand in, what to prepare for, or how to plan, for that matter. Year number two feels worlds better. Of course, how does all of this affect my teaching? How does it influence what goes on in my classroom? How do these values (time with family, balancing personal and professional needs, caring deeply for the young people I have the privilege to make mistakes with) color how I work to integrate into or change the fabric of the institution where I work?

These questions really spring, in my opinion, from the deeply personal nature of teaching. As I think about goals and priorities for my work, I find that these goals and priorities often cross over an increasingly fuzzy line between personal life and work. Issues of respect, community, responsibility, challenge, are all central to my work and my life. The exciting—and daunting—aspect of teaching for me is that it is an extension of who I am. And yes, as I enter my second year with only a limited repertoire of tools to carry out my work, I am keenly aware of the vulnerability that is teaching. Sure, there is a certain level of control that any good teacher has in the classroom. Ideally, students should be aware of each other by listening, helping, teaching each other. The fact is, though, that day after day, the teacher is "out there" in front of twenty to twenty-five individuals who are keenly observing the teacher in at least as many different ways. I try not to focus on this last realization because it might become too intimidating.

But what is the point of all this rambling? For me, what I bring to the classroom is not unlike what I bring to my family on a daily basis. Taking risks, learning how to respect one another, listening, having high expectations for oneself—these are all activities for which I hope to create a conducive environment in my classroom. In parallel with the different names that I use at home and at work ("Marco" and "Mr. Curnen," respectively), the packaging of my values in the two places is only slightly different.

In thinking about what I am writing, I am struck with the thought that these kinds of philosophical, overarching reflections don't seem to come up during the school year, just at the beginning and the end. Much of our time as teacher is spent honing our technical skills. Although technical skills are clearly important, I find that the students take with them more of the personal challenges and habits formed by these challenges than specific verb tenses, algebraic equations, or specific dates of this or that battle. How one creates and follows up on these kinds of lessons is the trick. I am far from an expert in this, but I hope to become more of an expert over the years.

The place where I work, for the most part, supports my vision for teaching. Certainly the institution provides it in many concrete ways: technology, support staff, copying machines, staff breakfasts, funding for professional development, and so forth. I find my work environment to be one of challenge. The staff, by and large, is held to and holds itself to very high expectations. I see my colleagues working quite hard. There is no doubt in my mind that I am part of a professional staff. The students are the beneficiaries of this environment, as they should be. After all, that is why schools exist and why I am inspired to try to be a teacher. I care about young people and their healthy development. I believe that Brookline High shares this concern. Supporting teachers goes a long way toward maximizing the potential that students take from their education.

So, as the days of the 6 A.M. wake-up loom ever nearer, I know that I, too, will go through a transition from a more individual, personal focus to a more community, outward focus. I will go from wearing shorts and a T-shirt to pants and a tie. At least one thing won't change: my mother-in-law will still correct my Spanish. This, of course, is significant: I am a Spanish teacher. And I am living proof of life-long learning.

But there are still more questions: How do I strive to influence the institution where I work? In what ways can I expect more from my colleagues as well as myself? One area where I believe schools can never do too much work is around building community. By this I mean bringing teachers from the same school (or system, if the school is unusually small) together to work through dilemmas, critique each other's work, and provide support through a deep understanding of one's classroom workings. I was lucky enough to be invited to take advantage of just such an opportunity as a first-year teacher, and I hope to continue to participate in this kind of professional development as much as possible for the remainder of my career.

This institutional support works in the following way: A group of experienced teachers from a variety of disciplines and backgrounds looks at a case study, a specific dilemma, provided by a colleague, who is the "subject" of that particular meeting. The dilemma may include a problem, an unusual situation, or just a way to gain an objective opinion on what is going on in one's classroom. The group listens, asks questions, and tries to identify what the question really is. Then, based on their experiences, each teacher provides a potential solution or tool. The "subject" is thus provided with an instant list of some fifteen to twenty possible solutions. From this list, it is suggested that one chooses two or three to try in the classroom. A meeting is then scheduled at a later date to provide time to try out the new methods and to then bring back results to the group.

Obviously, this is not my own idea. I just happened upon it because a caring colleague asked me whether I would be interested in participating in such a process. However, I believe this kind of activity holds great potential for institutional change. Unlike some professional development in-service days that feature "experts" imported to a school community, our support group is made up of teachers from the school. Although all of the teachers forming the group may not know every potential subject (especially in a large school), they at least work at the same school. This allows them to focus on the dilemma and not worry about tangential information such as scheduling restraints or physical plant limitations. These same teachers may very well know or have worked with some of the students with whom the "subject" is struggling. The suggested solutions are more powerful and relevant. Finally, since everyone involved in the process works at the same institution, the likelihood of follow-up is greatly increased. An outside group does not need to be rehired; instead, another meeting is planned at the end of the first meeting. Because teachers see each other in the hallways and in passing, the potential for further communication more around specific points is increased.

I take time to explain this process only to illustrate what, for me, represents a professional development tool that I hope to use and advocate on a consistent basis as my career unfolds. It keeps me healthy as a teacher, it builds community in what would otherwise be a potentially compartmentalized institution (Brookline High has close to 200 staff members), and it gives teachers the opportunity to learn from one another in a nonjudgmental way, free from the supervisor-supervisee hierarchy.

But as wonderful as this peer professional development group is, I find I need more. This is where the conflict arises. Do I, as an individual, work to bring about my own development, sometimes working against what feels like a never-ending bureaucratic chain-link fence, or do I expect—and demand—more support and space from my institution? This is a challenging, but essential, balance to strike. My professional growth is an area that I need to focus on consistently if I am to stay healthy as a teacher.

Brookline High definitely has plenty of room for improvement with regard to staff development. One obvious venue is in the common block planning and sharing time. Unfortunately, this all too often falls victim to scheduling constraints. The sheer size of our school seems to conspire to undermine any space or time for teachers from different academic and extracurricular areas to spend time learning from each other. Once we have retreated into the nine-month shell, it is so hard to break rhythms and rituals that we need to survive the rigors of the year. But we could all be so much healthier if we had some open time to reflect on our work, challenge each other, observe, and try something new. The students would most certainly benefit.

As I take this time to reflect back on my first year, I realize that one of the things I most fear—the vulnerability that comes about when one engages in a human relationship—cannot exist without one of the things that I most treasure: the moments when the human relationship matures. For me, these are my most treasured times as a teacher. Looking back at my journal from year number one and reading about the closing days in June when a specific student took time to tell me what she had learned from me, makes me feel like I could teach forever. Though I will always be able to improve my techniques, strengthen my classroom management, deliver a subject in a more fluid way, the relationships with students will always be paramount for me. After all, at the risk of delivering a cliché, these young people are human beings in need of care, compassion, limits, and love just like other human beings. It is no wonder that teaching is such an emotional job. I only wonder whether the bags under my eyes, or my gaunt exterior during the interminable winter months, are the prerequisites for success in June. I am confident that there are colleagues out there who will augment my personal learning by showing me some alternative pathways. So bring on the anxiety, dreams, and early-morning wake-ups! I am ready for year number two.

MARCO CURNEN *teaches Spanish at Brookline High School in Brookline, Massachusetts. Marco graduated from Williams College, taught for two years in a private school, and then worked in a community after-school program and a school-to-career program for adolescents in the Boston area. He continues to stay up late at night, after his two children have gone to bed, thinking of better ways to balance the responsibilities of teaching and parenting.*

Large schools move like icebergs that, once on course, resist the currents of change. In just such an environment, Morgaen attempted to teach for change but met with a host of barriers. Despite obstacles to innovation, she learned that with the proper attitude and allies, change can occur at glacial institutions. Change, no matter its dimensions, spawned hope and a growing sense of community for Morgaen.

6

Teaching and traditionalism: Encounters with "the way it's always been"

Morgaen L. Donaldson

I HAVE ENCOUNTERED challenges. I have felt sweat trace down my nervous back as I desperately tried to find my way in dark and unfamiliar cities. I have spent long hours deciphering texts in dank, obscure corners of college libraries. I have rebuffed a mob of drunken men reveling in the bachelor's celebrations that accompany traditional Hindu weddings in India. In windowless, foul rooms, I have shuddered and quaked in the throes of mysterious disease with only rodents to witness my agony. In my life, I have labored to complete difficult tasks, overcome self-doubt, and conquer personal inadequacies. But nothing, despite my experiences

NEW DIRECTIONS FOR SCHOOL LEADERSHIP, NO. 11, SPRING 1999 © JOSSEY-BASS PUBLISHERS

as a student and novice teacher, and no one, despite my matricula-tion at Harvard Graduate School of Education, prepared me for my first year of teaching.

Full of dreams, I accepted my first job teaching history at an urban-suburban high school in Framingham, Massachusetts. As a student teacher, I had worked in a progressive urban school that encouraged innovation while providing the support necessary to ensure its success. I chose Framingham High School because, although it adhered to the "traditional" model of a comprehensive secondary school, it offered autonomy in the classroom.

Additionally, I selected this school because it reflected national demographics and provided greater socioeconomic balance than its more affluent neighbors. To be honest, I also chose this job because it chose me; as one of the "dime-a-dozen" new social studies teach-ers, I felt I could not afford to be excessively selective.

Entering my first year, I was excited by the various challenges Framingham High School offered. There, I would teach the girl who had recently immigrated from Brazil *and* the Stanford-bound boy who had received a lifetime of private tutoring. I would ignite in my students, all students, a passion for examination of the world and their place within it. I would have kindred colleagues who chal-lenged students and adopted a variety of styles in their pursuit of this end. I also imagined I would enjoy the support of parents and the general assent of students. Retrospectively, I should have tem-pered my optimism and examined more closely the role I would play within this large, traditional school. Then again, I doubt I ever could have been fully aware or prepared prior to joining this com-munity.

Surprises, surprises

So what were the surprises I encountered at Framingham? First, I learned that bureaucracy often obstructs precisely the channels of communication it is designed to gird and clarify. Furthermore, I learned this blockage leads to a polarization of issues that spawns more difficulties. Particularly where resources are scarce, group members perceive matters dichotomously: good versus bad, and, more saliently, us versus them.

My introduction to this phenomenon came on the first day of school, when all the teachers district-wide congregated to ratify the contract. There I learned I would earn less than the principal had led me to believe and less than someone of my qualifications had received the previous year. Perplexed, I became indignant when one observant third-year teacher indicated that the first-year salary for 1997–1998 was less than that for 1995–1996. This first-year salary reduction, explained the fifty-five-year-old union president, served to increase the salaries of veteran teachers and administrators with more than ten years in the system.

This first encounter with the union, a large group wrestling over scarce resources, left a bitter residue. Had the more veteran teachers no foresight? Is not the union meant to safeguard the interests of the many, not the few, and to defend most vehemently the rights of its most vulnerable? After all, I paid the same amount in union dues as my colleagues with thirty years' experience. I left this meeting feeling isolated and discouraged about the community of educators I was poised to enter. Although I resisted judgment, I sensed an emerging theme: each one for oneself and, in a school community of over 2000, one is a very small number.

Nevertheless, I began the school year with an optimistic, ambitious attitude. I was eager to implement the lessons I had garnered student teaching in Boston, studying at Harvard, and, prior to that, teaching at a university in Thailand. In my first few weeks, I encountered the tangible by-products of bureaucracy: stacks of repetitive forms and endless meetings regarding this procedure and that student. In addition, I burdened myself by endeavoring to meet privately with my students, all 140 of them, after school. I wanted to establish more personal contact with them as well as gain greater understanding of their learning strategies and access to resources.

My second surprise materialized in October, when logistical pressures began to affect my pedagogy. Traveling between four rooms to teach five classes, I struggled to locate and retain enough desks and textbooks for all my students and enough chalk for myself. I also battled to manage classes of thirty and over, all the while berating myself as I forsook student-centered projects and authentic assessment and receded toward multiple-choice tests and lecture-style teaching. My gravitation toward this assessment style, which runs counter to my educational philosophy, indicated I was entering survival mode. By early October I felt overwhelmed and ineffectual; sleeping five hours a night, skipping lunch to finish work, and rarely engaging in conversations with my colleagues, I felt I was failing as a teacher.

Just when I needed support most, the system exacerbated my problems. Already overflowing, class sizes ballooned in late September and October as the guidance department crammed students into my classroom without regard, it seemed, for the chemistry or composition of the existing class. My department head directed me to "just say no" to additional students but, when I objected to the entrance of one student into a class of thirty, the guidance department responded a day later that "the principal wants him here." Sensitive to the situation, my department head argued to guidance and the principal that I already had several students with special needs and several students who spoke English as a second language; ultimately, he succeeded in his argument. To me, this small victory represented a glimmer of hope. Although I resented the fact that my singular objection failed to carry sufficient weight, I now knew that my department head would offer support if I asked for it.

October also introduced me to my third surprise: my first encounter with the pressures of suburban childhood and the politics of schooling. At open house, I became one parent's political scapegoat as he prosecuted me in front of forty other parents for setting vague expectations and, ultimately, depriving his daughter of an "A" in advanced placement history. I have never felt so grossly devalued or disillusioned in my life. All the twenty-hour days, all the proverbial blood, sweat, and tears I had poured into offering the best experience possible, dissipated in a few prosecutorial and polarized questions. This encounter plunged me into a deep malaise: why the hell was I doing this job, earning less than $29,000 a year to be assaulted by parents and strong-armed by guidance and the administration? For a month, I could not bear to listen to National Public Radio because the reports reminded me of all the other fascinating jobs I could have. Instead, I had taken a job at a school where teachers are cogs in the machine; people notice them only when they malfunction.

Comfort and solace

Open house, however, for all its affirmation of my worst fears, also provided me with a shade of hope. In my discontent and disillusionment, I did find certain people who offered initial support that grew to relationships of collaboration. A few people, mostly second- and third-year teachers themselves, stepped forward to give advice and share their own accounts of dealing with hopelessness derived from working in a factory where numbers take priority over people.

These relationships evolved in a way I needed, as a teacher and as a person. I needed mentors and I found them in colleagues whose experience most closely mirrored my own. Although Framingham had appointed me a veteran mentor, he showed little interest in nurturing my skills; a skilled pedagogue and true intellectual, he had learned the "hard way" and believed new teachers should struggle in Puritanical solitude. My philosophy, needless to say, opposed his diametrically. Our interactions point to the general superficiality of many mentoring programs: Did anyone ask this man if he wanted to be my mentor? Did anyone ask me if I felt he could support me? I assume he was goaded into the task—an example of educational fads reduced to their most skeletal, and potentially deleterious, forms.

Nonetheless, by the beginning of December, my feelings toward teaching and Framingham had progressed and improved. I was beginning to find people who struggled with the same questions that confronted me: How can I give each student adequate attention when my classes are so big? How can I teach in depth when state standards mandate I "cover" such a wide range of events and concepts? How can I experiment and push my students to question assumptions when I continually bump into systemic obstacles, in the form of directives, in my own practice?

In addition to voicing emerging questions, these supportive groups talked about kids! With great joy, we spoke about pushing them to explore and refine their ideas and supporting them when they crumbled under pressures and problems. Typically, these conversations germinated in the late moments of the day when everyone began to fill their briefcases with the night's work. Informal and often spontaneous, these interactions buoyed me in a time when I sensed imminent submersion. By the advent of second semester I was beginning to realize that I was not alone. Capable, committed people were very willing to help me, provided we had time.

Provided we had time. This, I began to understand, was the underlying barrier to innovation at Framingham High. The more I considered, the more I saw places where time and energy were spent unthinkingly and reactively, without a sense of purpose or connection to larger goals. Why, I queried the principal, do we have midterms, while continuing to teach and learn (or some semblance thereof) between hourly examinations?

He had no answer, except, "That's the way it's always been."

The way it's always been

"The way it's always been," a strange rejoinder for a school that has existed a mere six years. Entering a philosophical period, I began to consider how time affects learning and teaching at Framingham High School. As teachers struggle to "cover" material mandated by the state, and students scurry to complete work in the absence of study halls, there is a sense that time is perpetually "running out." Because adults and children here feel hurried and harried, time for reflection and thoughtful self-examination simply does not exist. Of course people follow "the way its always been." There is little time to consider alternative routes. Moreover, I began to realize that students and teachers alike found comfort in the status quo. A certain tacit collusion exists between adult and adolescent members of this community to perpetuate "how it's always been," whether the issue is school structure or pedagogy.

As I reflected on the cause of this orientation, I began to wonder how capable and socially committed adults, such as my informal mentors, could tolerate a system based on the default option, tradition, rather than a sustained, balanced inquiry. In the early winter, I wrote in my journal:

The sheer size of Framingham High School and those of similar dimensions sentences us to work in circles whose diameters rapidly shrink. In an effort to control our environs, we must reduce the range of our contact and, in doing so, the extent of our impact as individuals who desire change. Furthermore, we eliminate the "human element" of our environment. In the magnitude of this habitat, people become numbers or "problems" rather than humans. Is this the way we want our children raised?

A similar process happens with kids as they travel between teachers who do not know each other and classes that connect incidentally, if at all. I see fragmentation, isolation, and alienation, and, as by-products of these trends, a lack of respect for community, a lack of connection to the larger entity, and a dearth of personal responsibility. These latter trends translate into high drop out rates, vandalism, violence, and chronic rudeness on the part of various community members. *But can you blame these kids? Can you blame these teachers?*

My response to these trends was, in part, to rally a group of people who wanted to look critically and proactively at the mechanics of the school structure. A small group, we battled against complacency even more pervasive than it initially appeared. "This school," the principal told me when he offered me the job, "could be the best in the United States for educating a broad array of students." This mentality, manifested most obviously in frequent references to the fact that President Clinton signed the 1993 Educational Reform Act at Framingham High School, fosters complacency and rewards the status quo. Traditionalism prevails and innovation flounders in red tape as "an issue we're looking into." This big school moves like an iceberg; years pass before the course is altered even a degree, and past successes (or, arguably, avoidance of failures) reinforce the iceberg's tendency to retain its original sight.

The way it could be

So how does one first-year teacher attempt to slow and shift massive curricular and pedagogical traditionalism? First, I looked outside Framingham for the strength and inspiration vital to this effort. I returned to my friends from Harvard, who, as first-year teachers themselves, encouraged me to see myself as an agent of change. Invigorated and inspired by my friends' more objective perspectives, I began to throw myself into endeavors that supported my educational philosophy. Pursuing my desire to engage in self-reflection and evaluation, I joined the School Council, which brings students, parents, administrators, and teachers together. I also planned several projects to take students out of the classroom and into the community and coordinated several efforts to bring outside speakers into the school. These efforts required extra energy, but I needed them to give me hope, to see the larger impact of education on students and their world. We also set up weekly collaborative meetings among all teachers of American history, where we shared materials and effective strategies and considered the broader implications of our practice.

My resolutions and new involvement realigned my pedagogy and philosophy by emphasizing the connections between school and life. Initially, I had wanted to challenge students, to provoke them to take action, to cause them to sit up late at night wondering at the magnitude of the possibilities in the universe, and imagining their impact on each galaxy. Instead, the press of school machinery had forced me to teach them multiple choice and factual analysis; in truth, I wanted them to dream and create and stretch their minds and missions to shape the world. In January and February, I reminded myself of my original intent and recommitted to engaging students in an intellectual, moral, and emotional exploration of their place in society.

In the spring, I actively implemented my reinvigorated pedagogy. In one project modeled on the Revolutionary-era Continental Congress, two of my history classes exchanged letters criticizing Framingham's substitution of a one-week March vacation for the traditional two-week alignment. Embracing this issue, my students circulated a petition that eventually gathered over 400 signatures. In this instance and others, students began to take lessons out of the classroom, to seek me out at lunch with questions, to see me as an ally in their dual quest for knowledge and change.

As the school year hurtled toward its conclusion, I embarked on two projects that revolved around establishing creative and productive relationships among students, among teachers, and between students and teachers. First, I volunteered in an after-school program that united small groups of teachers and low-performing students to work on academics and social issues in a separate, supportive environment. Second, I collaborated with a photography teacher on an interdisciplinary project that united our classes to produce children's books on historical themes. This project culminated in a journey to a local elementary school, where our students read the books they had created to first graders. Both these endeavors demanded a lot of time and effort, but they took me out of the classroom to others' environments and to other schools. These were instrumental because they connected me to a larger community and reminded me that Framingham is a diverse and vibrant organism. In the same way, the interdisciplinary project took my students out of the classroom to apply their understanding of history in a different environment and through new media. In both undertakings, my relationships with students deepened and became more fruitful, for them and for me, on an intellectual and emotional level.

Last lessons

My final months at Framingham altered my impression of the school and demonstrated that change and innovation can occur at this glacial, conventional institution. In my spring successes, I caught a glimpse of the possibilities to help kids in high schools such as Framingham. My most emphatic and epiphanic realization was that to sustain my passion and energy, I needed to teach in accordance with my philosophy. Succumbing to the obstacles, or exaggerating their impact, began my spiral into despair. Furthermore, the unconventional teaching to which I naturally gravitated actually embodied change; the change had to begin with me, I realized, and in choosing to see the possibilities I began to teach in a manner that invigorated and inspired me. For me, this meant I needed to teach kids to question, I needed to form supportive and intellectually invigorating relationships with my colleagues, and I needed to take learning out of the classroom. Finally, I saw the change I sought to introduce to my environment, and I was overjoyed.

During the spring, I threw off the yoke of self-pity and began to scrutinize more impartially the workings of the school. Finally, in the spring, my vision refocused on the element that ultimately mattered most: personal, intellectual connections with students. I felt completely different than I had in October; now I was imparting something truly valuable, something more than dates and facts, an understanding more crucial than grammar and sentence structure. I was teaching students to teach themselves, giving them the tools with which to examine the world and their vital place within it.

With the perspective time and distance bring, I can more fairly assess Framingham's culture and curriculum. Serving 1900 students and an increasingly parsimonious pool of tax payers, Framingham High School struggles with the issues that confront many American high schools. Here, fundamentally good, intelligent people work to improve the lives of youth but are impeded in teaching to their full potential. What would enable new, progressive teachers to flourish in this environment? Fewer students, more time to plan, more flexibility, less pressure to conform to state frameworks of nebulous duration. More opportunity for collaboration built into the schedule. Higher expectations for all students, at all levels. More materials. More faculty representation at all levels of minori-

ties and women. Black History Month every month. *Smaller classes.*
More autonomy for teachers as well as input on schoolwide decisions. Attention to these issues will help avoid a situation that
caused me to feel, in the darkest period of my year, that I was doing
too much of what matters little and too little of what matters much.

It is November now, and I am well into my second year as a public high school teacher. Last spring, although classes were running
more smoothly and I had initiated several interesting projects, I
applied to a new, alternative public high school in the Boston public school system. I never expected to receive an offer, although I
prepared to the extreme for the interview. (This job has exposed
my compulsive, perfectionist character in a way that college and
graduate school never did.) In the end, I received an offer and
accepted. Who could refuse an opportunity to create a school, to
construct the curriculum and structure, and then participate in the
implementation?

My new school offers a radical contrast to Framingham; it is
small—160 students— and fiercely protects five hours a week for
teacher collaboration. I meet with the principal frequently, speak
with the guidance counselor several times a day, and communicate
with parents on a weekly basis. More important, I see my students
all the time, before and after school, and I observe their intellectual and emotional growth almost daily. Here, people, both adults
and children, talk about learning and the future. This school
embodies my final realization inspired by my first year of teaching. To nurture and develop new, progressive teachers, schools
need to support us and encourage us to teach in a manner that
brings us joy.

MORGAEN L. DONALDSON *teaches humanities at the Boston Arts Academy, a public high school for the arts in Boston, Massachusetts. During
the 1997–1998 year, she taught history, government, and global studies
at Framingham High School in Framingham, Massachusetts. She graduated from Princeton University in 1994, taught English at a university in Northern Thailand, and obtained a master's degree from Harvard
Graduate School of Education in 1997.*

All of us wish we had the opportunity to look back, hear from others, and ask, "What would I do if I had to do it all over again?" Myrna, a veteran principal, shares her reflections with us after reading the stories of the first-year teachers in this journal.

7

Leaders! Listen carefully to these hopes, these frustrations

Myrna Mather

I HAVE NEVER met these five young teachers, and yet I know them. Their stories are the stories of my colleagues, my friends, my partners in education, and they are my stories from thirty years ago. I feel privileged to have read their notes and reflections. They have bravely written their intimate and honest feelings about being a beginning teacher.

Their strong words demand that we as administrators and school leaders be as courageous as they have been. They compel us to ask ourselves, What can we do to serve our most hopeful, most vulnerable, and often most creative staff members? Can we serve them well enough before terminal disillusionment sets in and they leave the profession that so desperately needs them? Even more important, can we support and nourish the hope and enthusiasm that comes through clearly in their writing?

As I read the articles, certain phrases gave me a jolt, an unpleasant shock, a twinge of recognition and pain, but also a glimmer of

NEW DIRECTIONS FOR SCHOOL LEADERSHIP, NO. 11, SPRING 1999 © JOSSEY-BASS PUBLISHERS

hope and great satisfaction. They attest to the power of recording one's real feelings, of reflection, and of journal writing. Phrases are worth repeating, as they are a call to action for the principal in a school whose job it is to provide leadership and to set conditions necessary for learning. Real learning comes in partnership with adventure and imagination, questioning, guiding, and unshackling the mind. We often forget that—and it is often the new teachers who come with the ideals, bolstered by their recent training and by their fresh perspective on what we do.

These words from my five coauthors stood out for me:

Isolation ultimately undermines the will to press ahead despite the challenges posed.

Being a good teacher is not about following a recipe—it is about intellect and understanding, passion, empathy, patience, and dogged optimism.

I felt my mission was to go out and be an agent of change in the schools. I felt alone.

Teachers are like cogs in a wheel—people only notice them when they malfunction.

Schools overlook the challenge of complex thinking—it is easier to teach and learn on the surface. In an effort to teach the parts, schools destroy the whole, fragmenting it in order to polish and perfect each component.

I was doing too much of what matters little and too little of what matters much.

Although I found myself small and intimidated before the hugeness of the struggle to make education and life choices matter, it was the right struggle.

Teaching for me is an extension of who I am.

How do I strive to influence the institution where I work; in what ways can I expect more from my colleagues as well as myself?

I have gained more knowledge, more understanding, and more courage, not to mention a yearly love affair with at least 100 students.

Entering the teaching profession did not begin as a crusade to find my voice, although that is what it has become.

I keep re-reading these phrases, plucked from the journals of the young teachers in no particular order. Put together on one page, the message is powerful, and several themes emerge: isolation, vulnerability, loneliness, too much conformity, dishonesty, lack of encouragement, invisibility, frustration, the struggle with politics and bureaucracy; but also the love of students, the joy of connecting, and the magic of teaching and learning.

Each of these themes evokes memories of teachers I hired and labored with, sharing their frustrations and victories. They make me wonder, What would I do differently as a school leader if I had a chance to do it all again?

1. I would listen more and I would keep listening and encouraging new teachers to express their hopes and dreams and desires. In education we always are modeling for our staff and our students. We need to develop a relationship with them; giving young staff members your full attention whenever possible does much to reaffirm their sense of self-worth and encourage them to do the same with their students. The gift of complete attentiveness is priceless. One vice principal that I worked with always started the conversation with a student referred for bad behavior with this sentence: "I want to hear everything from your point of view no matter how long it takes," and he meant it. We as school leaders have to make the time to be present for those who are struggling and who need to be heard.

2. I would make professional dialogue and visits to classrooms a more visible part of my job and also part of the new teacher's experience. As one of our young writers said, "Teachers need professional camaraderie." We need to make it commonplace to visit each others' classrooms and engage in conversation about each others' struggles. Of course, it is part of that informal apprenticeship program that just makes sense for anyone learning his or her profession. All teachers need to value diversity in teaching styles and approaches, and value the controversy that may arise from this. School leaders can set the tone by sharing more of their own feelings and stories about teaching.

Schools should not be like hotels where no one knows or cares what is happening next door. This means finding opportunities for staff to share time and experiences. Taking over teachers' classes now and then would provide this opportunity for visits and also would remind us of our need to get back to our teaching roots. These experiences contribute enormously to building trust and community within the schools.

3. I would urge new teachers to speak often of their reasons for choosing teaching as a career. They need to go back to their vision of and idealism about becoming a teacher; too often in the everyday work of a teacher, these values become lost. Ask them to record their experiences, perhaps anonymously, and then make these required reading for those who run the school. After reading the journals of these five teachers, I am convinced that journal writing, the actual words on the page, will push us to make necessary changes in our schools. Encouraging educators to write of their experiences is often discouraging. A safe and trusting environment is a necessity. I have many times tried to get my own colleagues in our Principals' Centre to do this, and I meet with great resistance. We all need to be reminded that practitioner's writing is different from learned and research writing (the kind of writing that is usually associated with education). This "learned" writing is often not the kind of writing that is useful or friendly to daily practitioners. It is the practitioner's writing—writing that we do for ourselves— that can be the most motivating and the most insightful. You cannot make mistakes with practitioner's writing; the content belongs to the writer. Most important, it often speaks volumes to other practitioners.

4. I would encourage new teachers to come forward with ideas for school reform. It was delightful and a bit of a surprise to hear that these young people actually came into teaching with the goal of improving education, of participating in school reform. As much as possible, say "yes" more than "no" to their ideas, even if it means some inconvenience. Again we will be modeling what we want our students to do: experiment, take risks, change the world, and come to their own learning by trying and often failing.

I was particularly drawn to Allyson's words on voicelessness. I, too, in retrospect felt voiceless at school: "Somewhere, muddled in the lessons and beliefs of my teachers were my thoughts." It wasn't until I became a principal that I discovered a voice that felt like my own, because finally I was being asked to show some direction and provide some personal and professional leadership. This slow recognition of who I really am has haunted me all of my life and now I am realizing that a different kind of teaching will allow young people to discover who they are much earlier in their lives. Thank you Allyson for this reminder.

5. I would engage each young teacher in conversation early in the school year and ask, "What five things can I do for you this year that will make your job more rewarding?" Then I would say "yes" in some way to each of these and ask for something in return—a contribution that they can make, something that requires them to participate in teamwork for the good of the school.

6. I would give new teachers permission to make mistakes, along with an opportunity to talk and laugh about them, and, what is so important, permission to ask for help. How many times do we repeat the old truism that you learn by making mistakes? Yet we often do not tolerate mistakes easily in the educational system. Being right the first time gets the highest marks. Such a culture and system does not encourage learning in the deepest and most diverse ways.

7. I would reveal my own vulnerability more often. One day I received a note in my mailbox from the art teacher in my school. He was a teacher whom I often rescued from various situations with students and parents and head office, but the students loved and respected him deeply. In the note, he thanked me for my help for saving his skin yet one more time. He concluded with a line that has stayed with me: "I can sense in you an openness and a vulnerability that connects with me and my fears and weaknesses." As a manager I was tempted to be insulted by this comment, but as a leader it was indeed a compliment and I have always savored it as such. In it, he acknowledged my ability to support his learning, my giving him permission to ask for help without fear or shame.

8. I would keep this list of "woulds" in my daybook close at hand, easy to see, reminding me of my resolves daily.

When I was twenty and a first-year teacher, I never thought that I would one day be a principal. As that young teacher, I did not look to my principal for help. I felt the principal's role was to judge and measure and manage. But now I realize that principals have a big part to play in making young teachers believe in their work. This represents one of the essential changes over the years in the role of school leader—to be an empathic leader, one who inspires and serves.

Throughout my musings in writing this article, I kept thinking of two important obligations that we as leaders have: serving and modeling. By remembering to serve, we avoid the temptation to control and give orders. And by remembering to model, we remind ourselves, moment by moment, what leadership is all about. These two themes always brought me back to my real purpose in being a principal.

The first year of teaching can be difficult. There are doubts about having chosen the right profession. With self-confidence not yet established, decisions are often made to leave the profession prematurely. We need teachers as diverse as the students who are in their classes: the dreamers, the doers, the whimsical, and the serious. Students need that smorgasbord from which to graze and find their own passions and styles as learners and as people. For those who feel a real calling to teach, it is for us as administrators to smooth the way and be sensitive to what we can do for them. I sincerely hope that these five young and fearless teachers remain in the teaching profession, and I wish them a joyous journey in education.

MYRNA MATHER *recently retired as principal of Ursula Franklin Academy, Toronto, Canada, and continues to spark learning and good cheer among principals through her work at the Toronto Principals' Centre, University of Toronto/OISE, Toronto, Ontario, Canada.*

We often hear people draw analogies between education and the field of business. Rarely does the business of hair styling come to mind. Ross takes a close look at the experiences of first-year hair stylists and discusses what we might learn that could be useful in the schoolhouse.

8

Of hair stylists and master teachers

Ross Danis

I GET MY hair cut (styled) at a shop (salon) where my barber (senior stylist) gets more than the monthly cable bill to cut my hair and more than a lease payment on a Volkswagen Jetta for my wife. Is it worth it? All I can say is that a lot of people think so. One is considered fortunate to get an appointment less than a month in advance. Granted, everyone knows your name. Jennifer offers to take your coat and hang it up, Celeste gently massages your scalp, asking whether the water temperature is comfortable, and Cindy offers a cappuccino or Pellegrino with lemon. When Mark, my barber (senior stylist) arrives, he doesn't cut; he consults. We agree on what is about to happen before he begins to work (perform). During the haircut, one of the two owners stops by to observe what is taking place and to see whether everything is satisfactory. On the basis of the enormous success—and I mean enormous success—of this enterprise, the owners, Frank and Anthony, could qualify to lead virtually any Fortune 500 company.

NEW DIRECTIONS FOR SCHOOL LEADERSHIP, NO. 11, SPRING 1999 © JOSSEY-BASS PUBLISHERS

I am intrigued by the operation of this salon and by the very sophisticated business acumen of the owners. After all, there are hundreds of salons within a twenty-mile radius of my home. They range from the $8 Super-Cuts to the $25 La Mirage. Why are people, especially women, forking over ludicrous amounts of money for appointments months in advance, often at inconvenient times?

I started to request Frank, one of the two owners, for my haircuts. I wanted to know the secret. Frank explained that they only hire stylists with a "full book." This means that they already have experience and a following. When he hires a new stylist they do not just start cutting hair, they sweep the floor in the shop. Frank has them do this so they can look and listen to "how things are done at Frank-Anthony's—how to address clients, how to offer services, and how to deal with difficult customers." I asked Frank whether the new stylist then begins cutting hair. (After all, they know how and they know the expectations and the attitude of the shop.) "No. Then they shadow me or Anthony for six months," Frank replied. "We want them to just watch and learn." After this induction period, the new stylist begins cutting hair but not as a senior stylist. Senior stylists are in demand and can charge more for their services.

I probed further. "How does one become a senior stylist?" Frank explained that a large percentage of the operating budget is spent on training. Everyone is expected to go to New York to learn the latest cuts and color. Experts in the field facilitate regular demonstrations on Sunday mornings when the shop is closed. All employees are expected to attend. Both Frank and Anthony continue to refine their own skills as well as their understanding of the latest trends and products. They are students themselves, sharing videotapes and books with the staff. They just don't cut hair at Frank-Anthony's; this is a learning community.

After twelve months, each stylist performs a variety of cuts under the watchful eye of Frank or Anthony. If all goes well (and after a "meet and confer" that includes a discussion of attitude and skill), the title "senior stylist" is bestowed upon the proud employee. Even after clearing this milestone, continued employment is based upon continued participation in professional growth and development.

Frank and Anthony have devised a surefire way to employ superb hair stylists. What resemblance is there to the way we induct new teachers in most school districts? Teaching our children carries an enormous responsibility. Parents have entrusted the development of skills, dispositions, and habits of mind to our schools and ultimately to our teachers. Given the extraordinarily important role that teaching plays in the lives of children and adults and in the development of economies, social structures, and civilized cultures, what processes are in place to increase the probability of success of a new teacher?

The truth about being new

If you want to feel the genuine angst, frustration, and anomie that many new teachers experience, read the opening paragraph of Morgaen L. Donaldson's article in this journal. Paraphrasing, she indicates that she has been sick in foreign countries, has fended off drunken revelers, struggled through a prestigious university, and overcome personal challenges. None of these experiences, Morgaen indicates, prepared her for her first year as a teacher. Well, Morgaen, you should have become a hairdresser. Their sophisticated induction program could have increased the probability that your first year would have not left you feeling "grossly devalued" or "disillusioned."

Morgaen's story is not an exception to the typical experience of a new teacher, especially those with the highest competency and the greatest potential for making a difference within the institution and in their own classrooms. Allyson Mizoguchi writes, "In attempting to nurture my students' voices, I am inadvertently freeing my own." What are we, as administrators and as leaders, doing to help all of our teachers find their voices? How can we celebrate, nurture, and affirm these bright, fresh voices?

If left to chance, the only voice that will remain will be indistinguishable among the symphony of voices that echoes through the faculty rooms and hallways of our institutions. Those that carry an edge, or provide some dissonance, will be perceived as shrill, and will slowly fade away. Yet it may be that the voices that are calling out from the edges, those that we hear in the stories of new teachers, are the voices that will trumpet the rise of a school culture that stimulates the intellect, cultivates the spirit, and nurtures the soul.

If they only knew

If new teachers only knew how much hope and how much responsibility that administrators invest in them, they would be even more overwhelmed by their first-year experiences. This past school year, I was trying to orchestrate a major change in the way the primary grades are organized in our district. The structure was changed so that basal readers were phased out and replaced by a literature-based program. Classes were heterogeneously grouped so teachers could implement integrated units in flexible periods. One important piece of the change process was to transfer several teachers out of the first and second grades and hire new staff that represented a more natural fit with the new approach to teaching and learning.

Looking for key words and experiences such as "whole language" or "developmentally appropriate" philosophy helped screen letters of interest and applications. We carefully identified the dispositions that we felt were necessary to carry the program forward in this new, dramatic departure from what was traditionally facilitated in the district. Imagine these new teachers being hired, thinking that they were a match with the district, when the district was really hiring them to facilitate a change in philosophy at the school site.

Talk about setting someone up for a rocky ride! Not only does the administration want these new recruits to perform well; we want them to perform differently. We want them to sing a different song in a symphony of voices that are singing the dominant, age-old tune. In fact, they are being recruited in hopes that they will be the mentors, not the mentees—the senior stylists, not barbers or floor sweepers. And we expect all this while their energies concentrate on satisfying the lowest levels of Maslow's hierarchy of needs—safety, security, belonging. The expectation is for them to operate at the transformative level while they scramble for chalk and construction paper!

I hold such hope for the new hires' success, but hope just won't cut it (no pun intended). They get dropped into a culture without any preparation. I fear that they will succumb to the lure of the priests and priestesses of the faculty room, confessing the sins of their supervisor or principal. I fear that they will gravitate to the malcontent whose mission is to maintain equilibrium and protect the status quo. Again, I hope that they find a soulmate, a comrade in reform, a colleague or two that they can share a laugh or a tear with while bolstering each others' faith that they made the right decision with their choice of careers. How can schools increase the probability that the new teacher will have a successful experience that will allow them to serve the needs of the district, and our children, as well as their own need to be validated for their own unique contribution?

Lessons from the salon

Just as the licensed hair stylist is asked to "sweep the floor" for a period of time to find out "how things are done around here," new teachers should be hired for the district, not for a position in a classroom. Why not hire groups of new teachers in advance of the inevitable openings that arise in the organization? While waiting for a classroom, the district employee can be assigned to different teachers, at different levels, to assist and observe. The concept is not new; doctors are expected to perform a residency or complete an internship.

It is time to consider the same requirement for teachers. They can be assigned to classrooms so the regular teacher can receive professional growth opportunities that go beyond one or two days. This would help reduce the inconsistent implementation of the program by a series of different substitute teachers who do not have the same commitment, training, or responsibility. By the time the new teacher is assigned to a class, the administration will know his or her strengths and inclinations, skills and dispositions, thereby increasing the likelihood of a match between teacher and grade level, subject and school. If a match does not exist, it is not a catastrophe, but simply a matter of both parties thanking each other for the experience and parting company.

Shadow the master

In the hair salon described earlier, new stylists are required to be mentored by the owners. This way the owners of the shop are guaranteed that their vision is communicated clearly to the new stylists. Our schools assign mentors for a variety of reasons—and some are not as valid as others. I know of several situations in which the assigned mentor was the only one willing or available. In some cases the mentor embraces practices that the district is trying to move away from. Why not create laboratory experiences on a variety of levels and subjects staffed by a team that includes a staff developer, a teacher, and a content specialist? Stables of new inductees could be cycled through a program that would allow them to be the "teacher of record," but with a support team that builds a safety net around the new teacher, thus providing a foundation of content and pedagogy.

Exhibition-based contract renewal

After twelve months as a hair stylist at Frank-Anthony's, stylists are asked to perform a variety of cuts under the watchful eye of the owners. Their future success hinges upon the demonstration of clear and specific sets of competencies. This is a concept that could and should be applied to teaching professionals. Yes, different administrators observe teachers over the course of a school year and, yes, observations are written and conferences are held. Yes, contracts are awarded based upon agreement at a meeting among the observers.

But this is not the same as having a clearly defined rubric of skills and competencies that teachers are asked to demonstrate. For example, watching a teacher teach is different from saying, "I'd like you to demonstrate the proper use of cooperative learning, integrated instruction, and instructional technology in a series of lessons. We wish to observe you implementing the techniques associated with writer's workshop. Please model an effective assessment conference with a student. When you are through, we wish to see several artifacts from the past school year that will help you explain the supporting rationale that guides your thinking about teaching and learning." In other words, what our profession needs to do regarding the evaluation process is to shift from "watching, writing, and discussing" to "defining, performing, and reviewing." And these must lead to full professional conversations about developing new pedagogical skills and knowledge.

Career ladders

Currently, the only option for an outstanding teacher to advance in the profession is to leave the classroom and become an administrator. What a shame. At Frank-Anthony's, every employee can aspire to become and probably become a "senior stylist." If we apply the same concept to our schools, there could be several ways to validate the superior performance and the wisdom of experience. A career ladder that includes "lead teacher," "induction specialist," "peer coach," and "staff developer" would provide better orientation, anoint priests and priestesses, defrock others, and provide a career anchor that could reduce the potential for bitterness as good, quality professionals move through the system.

Expand life experiences

The very best teachers are not just sets of skills and techniques. They are fundamentally interesting and interested people. Yet what experiences are provided for teachers so that they remain connected, vibrant, interesting, and evolving human beings? Sure, staff development opportunities may be provided to learn about a new method, but teachers' willingness to be open to using the new method is shaped by their receptivity to change. This receptivity to change is not engendered by mandate, it is fostered by creating a culture that validates, nurtures, and expands experience.

I am much more interested in the travel experiences of new teachers or the books that they are currently reading, the antique cars that they are restoring, or the herb gardens that they are cultivating than their descriptions of how to write an instructional objective. I am absolutely convinced that if staff development in schools included a commitment to expanding life experiences, professionals would slowly be pulled into the flow of change. Yoga, poetry festivals, whale watching, Earth Watch, hiking the Appalachian Train, taking jazz piano, or attending a week-long institute on "The Dance of Tennis" is not fluff, but part of an organized and effective way to cultivate a learning community.

Can we talk?

I was presenting a workshop for new teachers a few weeks ago, and one young man must have been feeling especially comfortable in the setting, as he simply blurted out, "Being a new teacher sucks." I didn't know how to respond, partly because it was such a jarring statement to hear in such a setting. (I can hear it being said across a bar, among friends, but here?) I gave him credit for putting his feelings right out in the middle of the room. I had been noticing him working late into the evening on several occasions. I knew that his last evaluation by his supervisor had not gone well. I wanted to throw him a life preserver, a line that could pull him to safety, yet all I could muster was, "Well Justin, being a new teacher is certainly a challenge—our workshop on instructional strategies will help make that experience more positive."

What I really wanted to say was, "Yes Justin, being a new teacher can be an intellectual, emotional, spiritual, and physical roller coaster. What are we doing here? Let's just end this workshop and go somewhere where we can really talk." With any luck, the stories and experiences of Morgaen, Allyson, Brian, Kelly, and Marco will start a conversation about how our profession can nurture the spirit, cultivate the soul, and give voice to the very professionals who hold the keys to the future of our schools and our children.

ROSS DANIS *is currently the assistant superintendent of schools for the Randolph Township School District in northwestern New Jersey.*

Index

Back Issue/Subscription Order Form

Copy or detach and send to:
Jossey-Bass Inc., Publishers, 350 Sansome Street, San Francisco, CA 94104-1342

Call or fax toll free!
Phone 888-378-2537 6AM-5PM PST; Fax 800-605-2665

Back issues: Please send me the following issues at $25 each.
(Important: please include series initials and issue number, such as SL8.)

1. SL _____

_____

_____

$ _____ Total for single issues

$ _____ Shipping charges (for single issues *only;* subscriptions are exempt
from shipping charges): Up to $30, add $5^{50} • $30^{01}–$50, add $6^{50}
$50^{01}–$75, add $7^{50} • $75^{01}–$100, add $9 • $100^{01}–$150, add $10
Over $150, call for shipping charge.

Subscriptions Please ❑ start ❑ renew my subscription to *New Directions
for School Leadership* for the year 19___ at the following rate:

❑ Individual $52 ❑ Institutional $105
NOTE: Subscriptions are quarterly, and are for the calendar year only.
Subscriptions begin with the spring issue of the year indicated above.
For shipping outside the U.S., please add $25.

$ _____ Total single issues and subscriptions (CA, IN, NJ, NY and DC
residents, add sales tax for single issues. NY and DC residents must
include shipping charges when calculating sales tax. NY and Canadian
residents only, add sales tax for subscriptions.)

❑ Payment enclosed (U.S. check or money order only)

❑ VISA, MC, AmEx, Discover Card #_____ Exp. date_____

Signature _____ Day phone _____

❑ Bill me (U.S. institutional orders only. Purchase order required.)

Purchase order #_____

Name _____

Address _____

_____

_____

Phone_____ E-mail _____

For more information about Jossey-Bass Publishers, visit our Web site at:
www.josseybass.com **PRIORITY CODE = ND1**

OTHER TITLES AVAILABLE IN THE
NEW DIRECTIONS FOR SCHOOL LEADERSHIP SERIES
Rebecca van der Bogert, Editor-in-Chief